Mastering Internal Controls and Fraud Prevention

by
**The Association of
Certified Fraud Examiners (ACFE)**
Austin, Texas

The Association of Certified Fraud Examiners (ACFE)
is a world-wide provider of anti-fraud training and education,
with over 30,000 members and more than 100 chapters
worldwide, providing anti-fraud educational materials to
over 100 universities. The material in this course is licensed,
adapted and edited from ACFE's "How To Prevent Small
Business Fraud."

Design: Moss Design, Bethesda,

ISBN 1-884826-31-8

INTRODUCTION

Mastering Internal Controls and Fraud Prevention covers everything that you need to know for the internal controls and fraud prevention portion of the *Certified Bookkeeper* examination. If you take the optional open-book Final Examination at the end of this workbook, return the answer sheet to AIPB and achieve a grade of at least 70, then become a *Certified Bookkeeper* within 3 years, you will receive retroactively three (3) Continuing Professional Education Credits (CPECs) toward the *Certified Bookkeeper* continuing education requirements.

Whether you use this workbook to prepare for the national certification exam or only to advance your skills and knowledge, if you take the optional Final Examination and achieve a grade of at least 70, you will receive an AIPB *Certificate of Completion.*

Internal controls are defined in *AICPA Professional Standards, Vol. 1*, as "the plan of organization and all of the coordinate methods and measures adopted within a business to safeguard its assets, check the accuracy and reliability of its accounting data, promote operational efficiency, and encourage adherence to prescribed managerial policies." This course focuses on *safeguarding the company's assets.*

When you have completed this course, you should know how to help your company or clients:

1. install basic internal controls, including segregation of duties, for preventing employee theft of inventory and other noncash assets, the signs of such theft, and the schemes that are used to steal;

2. with the basics of background checks on applicants to reduce the likelihood of hiring employees who steal, how to insure or bond employees who have access to company cash, and how to segregate duties to minimize the chance of employee fraud or theft of cash;

3. install internal controls that prevent check fraud by employees or customers, how to spot counterfeit or altered checks, and the basics of check-fraud schemes;

4. internal controls that prevent credit card fraud by customers, and how to spot counterfeit credit cards; and

5. internal controls that prevent vendors from cheating you.

To get the most out of this course, we suggest the following:

1. Read the concise narrative of the course section that you are on.

2. Read the narrative again.

3. Take Quiz #1 at the end of each section to see what you have learned and what you need to review.

4. Take Quiz #2 at the end of each section to master any points that you may have missed.

Lastly, after completing the course, please take a moment to fill out the brief Course Evaluation at the back of this workbook (whether or not you take the final exam). It will be a great help to us in improving this and other courses.

Enjoy the course—and congratulations on taking a major step toward advancing your professional k`nowledge and career.

CONTENTS

HOW DISHONEST EMPLOYEES STEAL INVENTORY

Types of Noncash Theft

Although this section covers inventory, many of the risks and controls apply to other company property such as office equipment (computers, printers, etc.), furniture and other noncash assets. The most common methods of stealing inventory and other noncash assets are:

- Unconcealed larceny (open theft of physical assets)
- Falsified receiving and shipping reports
- Fraudulent shipments
- Fraudulent write-offs

Unconcealed Larceny

Unconcealed larceny, the most common kind of noncash theft, occurs when an employee steals company property and makes no attempt to cover the theft— i.e., by writing off the missing items as "damaged" or in some other way. The employee hopes that no one will notice that the goods are missing or, if they do, that no one will discover who took them.

Why daytime unconcealed larceny often is not reported

In many cases, employees steal inventory or other noncash assets openly, during business hours and in plain view. Coworkers often think nothing of it because most people assume that their friends and acquaintances are honest and have a legitimate reason for taking the equipment or merchandise.

Even if employees know that coworkers are stealing, however, they may not report it because they feel "loyal" to friends or see the world in terms of "management v. labor"; or, there may be poor channels of communication in the company or none at all; or employees may be part of the theft. Employees may not report thefts by a superior for fear of losing their jobs.

Shipping personnel may steal merchandise from outgoing shipments. If your company receives frequent complaints of short shipments, consider monitoring outgoing shipments. You may uncover theft or discover a procedural problem that should be corrected.

Unconcealed larceny during nonwork hours

Most employees try to hide their thefts by stealing after hours or on weekends when no one is around. They are often the employees who have keys to the warehouse(s) or storeroom(s).

Falsified Receiving and Shipping Reports

A warehouse employee falsifies a receiving report to cover his/her theft by recording a shortage or "defective" goods. Of course, this will result in a discrepancy between the receiving report and the invoice—the vendor bills for 1,000 units, but the accounts payable voucher is for 900 units.

Fraudulent Shipments

Or, the employee steals inventory by creating a fraudulent shipping report that results in the company unwittingly delivering its assets to the thief or an accomplice, which can result in the theft of large quantities of inventory. (This is covered in more detail below under "Creating and booking fictitious sales orders.") In retailing, the employee pretends to ring up the sale for an accomplice, or grossly undercharges for the item, then mails the stolen goods. In some cases, accomplices may return the stolen merchandise to convert it into cash.

Fraudulent Write-Offs

There are several kinds of fraudulent write-offs.

Forced reconciliation of accounts

Today, most companies use the perpetual method to record inventory so there is a running count of how much merchandise *should* be on hand. New items are booked when received; items sold are removed from the books. One of the simplest methods for stealing inventory and concealing the theft is forced reconciliation of the ledger Inventory account. When the items are stolen, the thief credits inventory and debits Cost Of Goods Sold to reduce the amount of inventory recorded on the books until the total is in line with the shrunken inventory on hand.

Altering inventory records

Employee Alice counts goods on hand each month and matches her count to the balance in the Inventory account. One month, there are 1,000 computers on hand. Alice steals 10 computers, leaving 990. In her physical count she still reports 1,000 on hand, matching the balance in the Inventory account and covering her theft.

Creating and booking fictitious sales orders

Employee David steals inventory by shipping it to accomplice Anne and creates paperwork to show that the shipped merchandise was sold to Anne. The fictitious sales order justifies the fictitious shipping order and conceals the theft. Dave can further conceal the theft by crediting Inventory and debiting Cost Of Goods Sold or debiting Accounts Receivable and crediting Sales for the fictitious transaction.

Because nonpayment might reveal the theft, perpetrators may conceal it by:

- charging the sale to existing subsidiary Accounts Receivable that are so large the cost will not be noticed;

- creating a bogus subsidiary Accounts Receivable;

- charging the sale to an overdue Accounts Receivable that will soon be written off, effectively making the stolen inventory;

- writing off the bogus receivable to Discounts And Allowances or Bad Debt Expense; or

- writing off the stolen inventory or other assets to accounts such as Inventory Shortage.

Writing off good inventory—then taking it

Employee Joe writes off good inventory as "scrap" and then is actually permitted to take the "useless" assets, which he sells to an accomplice at a greatly reduced price, or simply gives away.

Red Flags of Inventory Theft Schemes

The greatest danger that a company faces in the theft of inventory is having no centralized department for receiving and storing merchandise. Thus, if theft is occurring, there may be no way for anyone to discover it.

The following irregularities may indicate inventory theft:

- ❑ Frequent customer complaints about shipment shortages.
- ❑ Employees frequently entering a warehouse or stockroom after hours or on weekends.
- ❑ High levels of inventory shrinkage.
- ❑ Unsupported alterations or adjustments to perpetual inventory records.
- ❑ Excessive purchases of materials or merchandise.
- ❑ An increase in the Cost Of Goods Sold as a percentage of sales.
- ❑ Shipments of merchandise for which there is no record of a sale.

❑ An increase in the number of uncollectible sales or in bad debt expense.

❑ Shipping records showing an employee's or competitor's address.

❑ Sales canceled after merchandise was shipped.

❑ Altered shipping tickets.

❑ Evidence of underbilling for shipped merchandise.

❑ An end-of-month balance in Inventory that differs from the next month's beginning balance.

❑ Projects that generate excessive materials costs.

❑ Purchases that cannot be traced to inventory.

❑ Purchases paid at full price for shipments tagged as having missing or defective merchandise.

❑ High levels of inventory written off as lost or stolen or as scrap.

❑ No recorded proceeds from the sale of scrap normally sold by the organization.

Five Internal Controls for Preventing Theft of Inventory

Effective controls must include detailed, written instructions for taking inventory and periodic review of these instructions. The instructions should include the following controls:

1. **Proper documentation properly monitored.**

❑ Written procedures on exactly how inventory is to be physically recorded.

❑ Pre-numbered and controlled:

- requisitions;
- receiving reports;
- inventory tags;
- perpetual inventory records;
- sales tickets;
- receipts;
- raw materials requisitions (for manufacturers);
- shipping documents;
- job cost sheets.

❑ Matching of all shipping documents to sales tickets.

❑ Investigation of shipping documents not associated with a sale.

❑ Matching of support documents before paying bills.

2. Established systems for storing and counting inventory.

❑ Practical ways to identify and describe inventories—e.g., permitting the person who counts the inventories to write "55 TVs" is so imprecise that it leaves room for a dishonest employee to substitute less expensive models for more expensive ones and cannot be reliably checked against purchase orders and receiving reports. <u>Better</u>: "55, 17-inch RCA flat screen TVs., Model 3400X."

❑ The method used to determine quantities.

❑ Exactly how inventory is to be physically recorded.

❑ Instructions on how missing, unused or voided tags are to be accounted for.

❑ Clear documentation of any special counting procedures such as volume conversions (converting liters to quarts, meters to feet, etc.).

❑ Procedures for counting work-in-progress inventory (for manufacturers).

❑ Careful identification and segregation of obsolete, slow-moving or damaged inventories.

❑ Periodic physical counts of all storeroom or warehouse stocks reconciled against perpetual inventory records *by someone other than the employee responsible for inventory records* to spot larger than normal shrinkage.

❑ Periodic physical counts of all storeroom or warehouse stocks at all locations, no matter how remote, matched against perpetual inventory records to spot larger than normal shrinkage.

❑ Procedures to prevent double-counting. In a large company, or in a small firm with large quantities of items, counting the entire inventory may not be practical, so spot checks are used instead. There must be mechanisms to mark all boxes containing inventory and to make sure that warehouse employees never know the order of the spot checks. Otherwise, there is the possibility that dishonest employees can take the same inventory and move it around so that it is double- or triple-counted during a spot check.

❑ Recounts of merchandise that is of substantial value.

❑ Checking of reductions in the perpetual inventory account against sales invoices.

❑ Checking that all the reductions in perpetual accounts are explained by source documents, such as sales invoices and approvals of any inventory, or spoilage being moved to scrap.

❑ Checking of increases in perpetual inventory records against source documents such as receiving reports.

3. **Segregation of duties.** The following duties should be handled by different personnel when possible:

❑ Procedures for authorizing purchases (and in some companies, sales).
❑ Requisition of inventory.
❑ Receipt of inventory.
❑ Control of physical inventory.
❑ Disbursement of inventory.
❑ Conversion of inventory to scrap.
❑ Receipt of proceeds from disposal to scrap.
❑ Spot checks by supervisory personnel.
❑ Independent checks of inventory by someone knowledgeable about the inventory but independent of the purchasing or warehousing functions.
❑ Physical control of inventory.
❑ Counting and valuing inventory.
❑ Recounting inventory.
❑ Recounting merchandise of substantial value.

4. **Physical safeguards.** Restrict as much as is practical the number of employees who have keys to the premises; this will help to reduce crime, but not to eliminate it because it is often committed by long-time, highly trusted employees. Physically lock up and guard all merchandise that is of high value or that can easily be converted into cash and limit access to authorized personnel. For example, placing security guards strategically may help to detect and deter theft schemes. Electronic devices such as cameras and surveillance equipment may also be used. But these devices will be effective only if the employee who handles them knows and adheres to physical-control procedures.

5. **Analytical reviews.** An analytical review measures specific changes in selected accounts and their related accounts over a given period. For example, take Sales and Cost Of Goods Sold, two accounts used by thieves. During a one-year period, 200X, Cost Of Goods Sold increases by 20%, but Sales increases by only 2%. The discrepancy may be due to increases in the cost of materials, intense competition or a major loss of market share. But if none of these factors changed in 200X, why did Cost Of Goods Sold increase at 10 times the rate of Sales? The possibility of stolen inventory and altered records should be investigated. An analytical review may also:

❑ Compare the current period's gross-margin percentages (net sales – cost of goods sold ÷ net sales) to those of prior periods for potential over- or understatement.

❏ Compare the current year's inventory turnover rate (cost of goods sold ÷ average inventory) to previous years.

❏ Compare current costs per unit to those of previous periods and years.

Which Employees May Be Likeliest to Steal

Experience shows that certain kinds of employee discontent may be hints of current or imminent employee fraud. This applies not only to theft of inventory but to check theft, misappropriation of funds involving credit cards and all other kinds of theft or embezzlement. While almost all employees at some time get angry at their employer, complain about being underpaid or have other resentments, deep-seated resentment may bear monitoring by management. Such resentment includes constant complaints by employees that they have been wronged by the company—e.g., being passed over for a promotion that they thought they deserved or not getting a raise.

Other signs that bear watching include deep dissatisfaction with or ongoing complaints about home life; an inexplicably lavish lifestyle; a problem with gambling, alcohol or drugs; or frequent calls from creditors. Unless the employee is in your department, take no action. Instead, report your concerns to management. In addition to being aware of employees who exhibit these signs, management may also want to further segregate some of their duties. The typical factors that can add up to an employee stealing are:

1. an insolvable problem;

2. a way to steal the items; and

3. the ability to justify the theft to him/herself.

QUIZ 1   HOW DISHONEST EMPLOYEES STEAL INVENTORY

Problem I.

Mark each statement True or False.

1. If company policy is to permit employees to take home damaged goods or scrap, there is no need to examine goods marked "damaged" or "scrap" that employees are taking home.

     a. True   b. False

2. One way to discover fraud is to compare cost per unit for the current year against that of previous years.

     a. True   b. False

3. If you are looking into missing inventory and find both the sales order and shipping document for that inventory, then you know that no inventory has been stolen.

     a. True   b. False

4. One way to discover fraud is to compare net profit for the current year against that of previous years.

     a. True   b. False

5. Fraud may sometimes be revealed by applying the current-year inventory turnover ratio to prior years, which is computed as follows: cost of goods sold ÷ sales

     a. True   b. False

Problem II.

1. What are the five overall internal controls for inventory?

a.

b.

c.

d.

e.

2. Name five kinds of accounts that a dishonest employee might use to conceal nonpayment for stolen inventory?

a.

b.

c.

d.

e.

3. Which two kinds of inventory should be carefully identified and segregated to prevent their being stolen or to discover if they have been stolen?

a.

b.

QUIZ 1 Solutions and Explanations

Problem I.

1. False.

One way dishonest employees steal is to mark salable inventory or other company assets "damaged" or "scrap" in order to steal them.

2. True.

3. False.

You need to check whether the person to whom it was delivered actually paid for the inventory, since he or she could be a dishonest employee's accomplice and both the sales order and shipping documents could be fraudulent.

4. False.

The current-year figure to compare against prior years is gross margin percentages.

5. False. Cost of goods sold ÷ average inventory.

Problem II.

1.
 a. proper documentation, properly monitored
 b. systems for storing and counting inventory.
 c. segregation of duties
 d. installation of physical safeguards
 e. analytical reviews.

2.
 a. a very large subsidiary Accounts Receivable
 b. an overdue Accounts Receivable
 c. Discounts And Allowances
 d. Bad Debt Expense
 e. Inventory Shortage

3.
 a. slow moving inventory
 b. damaged inventory

QUIZ 2   **HOW DISHONEST EMPLOYEES STEAL INVENTORY**

Problem I.

Multiple choice. Circle the correct answer.

1. When discussing fraud, forced reconciliation refers to . . .

    a. the bookkeeper being compelled to reconcile the ledger Cash account to the bank statement.

    b. the balance in the Inventory account being falsified to reflect goods on hand after inventory has been stolen.

    c. a practice that is no longer possible with today's computerized accounting.

    d. when the ledger Sales account is falsified to equal the balance in the Cash account.

2. The employee likeliest to steal by using keys to company premises is the employee who has the keys to do his or her job and . . .

    a. is a long-time, trusted employee

    b. has an unsolvable problem and a way to steal

    c. can justify the theft to him/herself

    d. all of the above

3. The reason that employees may not report coworkers whom they see taking inventory or other noncash assets is that . . .

    a. they assume the coworker has a valid reason for removing the item(s).

    b. they want to be loyal to their friends at work.

    c. they see the workplace in terms of management v. labor.

    d. all of the above.

4. Which of the following is a red flag of inventory theft?

    a. an increase in the cost of Inventory as a percentage of Sales
    b. an increase in Inventory as a percentage of Cost Of Goods Sold
    c. an increase in Accounts Receivable as a percentage of Sales
    d. a decrease in Cost Of Goods Sold as a percentage of Sales

5. Which of the following is a red flag of inventory theft?

    a. an increase in uncollectible sales
    b. an increase in bad debt expense
    c. an increase in sales being canceled after they are shipped
    d. all of the above

Problem II.

Name the five key components of good internal controls for inventory (yes, this is a repeat of the question in Quiz 1 because it is important information).

    a.
    b.
    c.
    d.
    e.

QUIZ 2 Solutions and Explanations

Problem I.

1. b
2. d
3. d
4. d
5. d

Problem II.

a. proper documentation, properly monitored
b. systems for storing and counting inventory
c. segregation of duties
d. installation of physical safeguards
e. analytical reviews

This page left blank intentionally.

HOW TO PREVENT—OR SPOT—EMPLOYEE THEFT

Select the Right Employee

A key step in preventing employee fraud is deciding whom the company will employ. Whether the time and expense of background checks is worth the return is up to the company.

At a minimum, the company should check the background of any employee who will have constant access to cash, checks, credit card numbers, inventory, or any other items easily stolen.

Before hiring, check as many of the following as possible:

- **Past employment.** Even though most employers will verify only position and dates of employment, their tone of voice may reveal what they think of the employee. Also, ask previous employers whether the applicant is eligible for rehire. A more aggressive question (and therefore less likely to be answered) would be: "If you were me, would you hire this person?"

- **Criminal convictions.** Services such as Nexis and ChoicePoint have criminal conviction records for almost every large county in the U.S. If these services do not include the candidate's former or current county of residence, the company can go to that county's courthouse and check the criminal courts division's criminal records.

- **Drug screening.** Many firms screen potential hires and current employees for drugs. Frequent drug users may be more prone to theft or fraud.

- **References.** An astonishingly small number of employers actually call a candidate's references on the assumption that a former supervisor or coworker will give a good reference so calling is a waste of time or that no applicant will give them a bad reference. But applicants can and do list important-sounding false references hoping that no one will call them.

- **Degrees, certifications and licenses.** Always verify a candidate's educational degree, license, or other certification with the school or issuing organization. It is not unusual for someone to claim a certification or license that has been revoked in a disciplinary action. Most licensing or certification organizations, including the Association of Certified Fraud Examiners, will tell you if any disciplinary action has been taken against the person.

Get the Candidate's Consent

Numerous federal laws (such as the Fair Credit Reporting Act) and state laws govern the gathering and use of information for pre-employment purposes. Many require a candidate's written consent to obtain this information. Even when not required, it is advisable to get the candidate's signed authorization and release. Thus, it is *essential* that the company consult human resources and/or legal counsel about laws and regulations that may apply to:

1. requesting a candidate's authorization to seek the information or to give a drug test;

2. the wording of the authorization or release that a company is asking the candidate(s) to sign; and

3. procedures for dealing with rejected candidates if the information obtained was used to make the hiring decision.

Audit for Fraud

In a small company, the audit can be done by the owner, bookkeeper (only on records not kept by the bookkeeper), or outside CPA. It consists of checking for authorized purchases and sales and other high-risk areas and reviewing controls for vulnerability to fraud or if fraud has occurred—e.g., sales numbers do not match inventory numbers. The audit must be conducted by someone other than those who normally handle the following records and should include:

❑ Expense reports.

❑ Payroll records.

❑ Purchasing records, including:
- ✓ purchase requisitions;
- ✓ purchase orders;
- ✓ receiving reports;
- ✓ vendor invoices; and
- ✓ subsidiary accounts payable ledgers.

❑ Sales records, including:
- ✓ customer orders;
- ✓ shipping documents;
- ✓ sales invoices;
- ✓ remittance advices; and
- ✓ Subsidiary accounts receivable ledgers.

❑ Accounts receivable.

❑ Customer complaints.

❑ Cash records.

❑ Suspense accounts.

Theft Insurance:
The Fidelity Bond

Many organizations, from the one-employee startup to giant corporations, carry insurance policies against fraud in the form of a *fidelity bond*, generally referred to simply as "bonding."

A fidelity bond covers every kind of loss from routine theft and embezzlement to commercial bribery and stock fraud. If a customer sues your company for failure to deliver stolen goods or for other reasons related to the bonded employee's dishonesty, the insurance will cover defense costs. The bond may also cover loss of earnings sustained as the result of theft of the company's customer, applicant or employee lists.

Optional coverage may include losses from:

- counterfeit paper currency or money orders;

- forged deposits;

- forged credit cards; and/or;

- computer forgery.

The burden of proof is on your company to show that the fraud caused the losses claimed and does not reimburse unexplained inventory losses or pilfered cash accounts without a suspect.

Fidelity bonds almost always include a *subrogation* provision. Subrogation requires that, if the insurer pays your company's claim, your company . . .

- gives the insurer the right to sue the wrongdoer;

- cannot interfere in any way with the insurer's right to sue; and

- cannot agree to any settlement with or release of the dishonest employee unless the insurer consents.

The insurer may sue to recover, in addition to the insured losses covered by the fidelity bond, the *uninsured* losses suffered by your company that exceed the policy's coverage.

Your company will receive any amount recovered in excess of the policy's coverage.

Signs of Employee Fraud or Theft

If you see any of the following signs of trouble, alert management immediately:

- Employee checks (especially postdated ones) are found in the cash drawer during the cash count.

- A spike in employee complaints about W-2 errors.

- High turnover in a particular department.

- A department's requests for more staff unrelated to an increase in workload or other causes.

- Checking accounts are not reconciled regularly.

- A big, inexplicable increase in sales returns.

- Unusual bad-debt writeoffs.

- Unusually slow collections.

- A noticeable unexplained decline in cash sales or a disproportionate increase in credit sales.

- Unusual drops in revenue or increases in expenses.

- Deposits in transit are growing or are slow in reaching the bank.

- Collection of past-due or written-off accounts becomes unusually lax.

- An increase in past-due accounts, customer complaints about prior payments not being credited to their account, excessive late charges, or increases in the number of late charges being written off.

- The general ledger trial balance does not balance or computer journal entries in subsidiary accounts do not equal control-account totals.   <u>For example</u>, A/R is $100,000, but total subsidiary ledger accounts total $96,000. This may indicate that an employee kept or "borrowed" $4,000 by crediting an A/R subsidiary account. Savvy hackers can even do this on sophisticated accounting software.

- Employees have made entries or adjustments to their own accounts.

- Orders are entered late in the reporting period by the rep, then canceled.

- Discounts are unusually large.

- Payees have common addresses.

- Files contain copies of invoices, not originals.

- Too many company checking accounts (can be used for kiting).

- Excessive or unjustified cash transactions.

- Assets are sold but are still on the premises.

- Assets are sold for less than their fair market value.

- Dramatic, unexplained changes in financial ratios.

Controls Against Employee Fraud in a Very Small Company

Even a firm with just one or two employees can protect itself against employee fraud.

Involve the spouse

A spouse not involved in the business can still help with internal controls, according to Professor David P. Kirch, CPA, PhD of the University of Ohio. For instance, consider using the owner's address for all tax-related correspondence and having monthly bank statements sent directly to the owner's home. Advise the owner to open the bank statement and shuffle the contents before bringing it to the office.

Employees who may see the bank statement will know that someone else has reviewed it, but not know how closely or what was reviewed and are likely to assume that there are more controls than there actually are.

Because a spouse who hears the owner discuss daily business operations will pick up internal control problems of which the owner is not aware, he or she should be at the first meeting where internal controls are discussed. Spouses tend to be much less trusting of employees than owners, especially when workers are the same sex as the spouse. Spouses also tend to be curious and might ask questions about an expense or authorization that conveys to employees who deal with financial items that revenues, expense, purchase orders, etc. are being reviewed.

But a spouse working at the firm presents special problems. Normal controls may be relaxed or ignored because of the owner-spouse relationship. When the spouse retires or leaves for other reasons, the relaxed controls are inadvertently passed on to his or her replacement, giving that person an easy way to steal. The relaxed controls over the replacement may then seep into other, more sensitive areas where the spouse was never involved. Therefore, when setting up internal controls, ignore the fact that an employee is a spouse.

QUIZ 1   HOW TO PREVENT—OR SPOT—EMPLOYEE THEFT

Problem I.

Fill in the blanks.

The following questions apply to applicants for jobs in which they will have constant access to cash, checks, credit card numbers, inventory, or any other items easily stolen.

1. Regardless of whether an applicant's past employer is willing to give more than past position and dates of employment, it is a good idea to ask whether the applicant is eligible for _____.

2. Two commercial services that have criminal convictions for almost all counties are _____ and _____.

3. If a commercial service does not have criminal conviction records for the county where a job candidate lived or worked, you can check the records at that county's _____, where you would look at the _____ _____ division's criminal records.

4. Always verify a candidate's _____ _____, _____, or _____ with the issuing institution—and, where appropriate, ask if any _____ _____ has been taken against the person.

5. It is very important to obtain a job candidate's _____ _____ to check references or any other part of the applicant's background.

6. An effective control in a small company is to have the monthly bank statement sent to the owner's _____ address to be reviewed, or at least to have the cancelled checks shuffled.

7. Spouses involved in internal controls tend to be much (more/less) trusting of employees than owners, especially when workers are the (same/different) sex as the spouse.

8. When setting up internal controls, you should (take into consideration/ ignore) the fact that owner's spouse is an employee.

Problem II.

1. Check each of the following that are signs of possible fraud and that you should make management aware of:

❑ A noticeable, unexplained increase in cash sales or a disproportionate decline in credit sales.

❑ A noticeable, unexplained decline in cash sales or a disproportionate increase in credit sales.

❑ A department's requests for more staff unrelated to an increase in workload or other causes.

❑ Bank deposits with checks for amounts that do not appear on the cash register tape or in other records.

❑ Unusual increases in revenues or drops in expenses.

❑ An increase in past-due accounts, customer complaints about prior payments not being credited to their account, excessive late charges, or increases in the number of late charges being written off.

❑ Collection of past-due or written-off accounts becomes unusually intense.

❑ Collection of past-due or written-off accounts becomes unusually lax.

2. Check each of the following that are signs of possible fraud and that you should make management aware of:

❑ Orders are entered late in the sales period by a rep, then canceled.

❑ Discounts are unusually small.

❑ Discounts are unusually large.

❑ Different payees have common addresses.

❑ Files contain copies of invoices, not originals.

❑ Assets are sold for less than their fair market value.

❑ Assets are sold for more than their market value.

❑ Excessive or unjustified cash transactions.

❑ Assets are sold, but are still on the premises.

❑ Dramatic, unexplained changes in financial ratios.

Problem III.

1. Name eight categories of records that should be checked in a fraud audit.

a.	e.
b.	f.
c.	g.
d.	h.

Problem IV.

Multiple choice. Circle the correct answer.

1. When a company insures itself by taking a fidelity bond on an employee, which of the following are covered?

    a. routine theft

    b. embezzlement

    c. bribery

    d. damages and defense costs resulting from the dishonesty

    e. all of the above

2. Which of the following may also be covered by a fidelity bond?

    a. counterfeit paper currency or money orders

    b. forged deposits

    c. forged credit cards

    d. computer forgery

    e. all of the above.

3. To collect reimbursement for losses under a fidelity bond a firm must. . .

    a. simply submit the losses to the insurance company.

    b. prove only that the fraud caused the losses claimed.

    c. only produce a suspect.

    d. prove the fraud caused the losses claimed and produce a suspect.

4. A subrogation provision in a fidelity bond requires that if the insurer pays your company's claim, your company . . .

    a. gives the insurer the right to sue the wrongdoer.

    b. cannot interfere in any way with the insurer's right to sue.

    c. cannot agree to any settlement with, or release of the dishonest employee unless the insurer consents.

    d. All of the above.

QUIZ 1 Solutions and Explanations

Problem I.

1. rehire
2. Nexis, ChoicePoint
3. courthouse, criminal court
4. educational degree, license, certification, disciplinary action
5. written consent
6. home
7. less, same
8. ignore.

   Otherwise, when the spouse retires or leaves for other reasons, the relaxed controls may inadvertently be passed on to his or her replacement, giving that person an easy way to steal.

Problem II.

1.
- ☑ A noticeable, unexplained decline in cash sales or a disproportionate increase in credit sales.
- ☑ A department's requests for more staff unrelated to an increase in workload or other causes.
- ☑ Bank deposits with checks for amounts that do not appear on the cash register tape or other records.
- ☑ An increase in past-due accounts, customer complaints about prior payments not being credited to their account, excessive late charges, or increases in the number of late charges being written off.

2.
- ☑ Orders are entered late in the sales reporting period by a rep, then canceled.
- ☑ Discounts are unusually large.
- ☑ Different payees have common addresses.
- ☑ Files contain copies of invoices, not originals.
- ☑ Assets are sold for less than their fair market value.
- ☑ Excessive or unjustified cash transactions.
- ☑ Assets are sold, but are still on the premises.
- ☑ Dramatic, unexplained changes in financial ratios.
- ☑ Collection of past-due or written-off accounts becomes unusually lax.

Problem III.

    a. Expense reports
    b. Payroll records
    c. Purchasing records
    d. Sales records
    e. Accounts receivable
    f. Customer complaints
    g. Cash records
    h. Suspense accounts

Problem IV.

1. e
2. e
3. d
4. d

QUIZ 2 HOW TO PREVENT—OR SPOT—EMPLOYEE THEFT

Problem I.

Multiple choice. Circle the correct answer.

1. Where would you find out if a job applicant had any criminal convictions?

    a. the county motor vehicle bureau
    b. the county courthouse, criminal records division
    c. the county courthouse, family division
    d. the county courthouse, district attorney's office

2. The references provided by an applicant . . .

    a. should be carefully checked.
    b. are a waste of time to check because applicants give only supervisors and coworkers who will give a good reference.
    c. should be evaluated by the importance of the position the person holds rather than by contacting the person.
    d. will always prevent you from hiring the wrong person.

3. Which of the following should be verified with the issuing institution?

    a. educational degrees
    b. licenses
    c. certifications
    d. disciplinary actions against the individual
    e. all of the above

4. Which of the following would be checked in a fraud audit?

    a. purchase orders against sales tickets
    b. shipping orders against sales tickets
    c. receiving reports against sales tickets
    d. sales orders against purchase orders

5. In a very small company, effective controls include . . .

    a. having the bank statement sent directly to the owner's home.
    b. having tax correspondence sent directly to the owner's home.
    c. establishing internal controls that include a spouse-employee.
    d. all of the above

Problem II.

Fill in the blanks.

1. To protect against fraud by an employee, the employer would take out an insurance policy known as a ＿＿＿ ＿＿＿, which is also referred to simply as ＿＿＿.

2. If a company insures against fraud, the burden of proof is on the company to show that the fraud caused the ＿＿＿ claimed, and there will be no reimbursement unless the company presents a ＿＿＿.

3. Subrogation gives the insurer the right to sue the wrongdoer and prevents the company from offering any ＿＿＿ or ＿＿＿ to the wrongdoer.

4. If the insurer sues the individual(s) involved in theft or embezzlement and recovers losses above the limits covered by the theft insurance, these amounts are kept by the (insurer/company).

QUIZ 2 Solutions and Explanations

Problem I.

1. b
2. a
3. e
4. b
5. d

Problem II.

1. fidelity bond, bonding
2. losses, suspect
3. settlement, release
4. company

This page left blank intentionally.

Section 3
CHECK FRAUD

Introduction

An estimated 1.2 million worthless checks go into the banking system daily, with losses of $50 billion a year from various check frauds. This amount will grow due to factors such as the increasing ability of desktop publishing, laser printers, and color copiers to make duplication and forgery more accurate and harder to detect and the fact that bad check passers move constantly, making prosecution still more difficult. Law enforcement's focus on violent crime and its displeasure at merchant attempts to use the police as check collection agencies result in 75% to 90% of check fraud cases never being pursued.

Types of Check Fraud

There are several types of check fraud. The first two below are the simplest and most common:

1. **Checks written on insufficient funds.** In many states, a check issued on insufficient funds—intentionally or not—is considered *prima facie* evidence of check fraud. *Prima facie* evidence means that the evidence gives a strong enough *appearance* of intent to defraud to take legal action against the check issuer even if no motive has been established and there is no indication that the check passer would not have made good on the check.

2. **Checks written on an account that the check passer knows is closed.**

3. **Counterfeit checks.** Although counterfeiters go to great lengths to make their checks look genuine, there are a few giveaways. Ways to spot counterfeit checks are found on page 29.

4. **Forgery involving your company's checks.**

5. **Employee theft involving vendor checks.** The dishonest employee opens an account in the name of the company at a different bank. When a vendor check arrives for, say, $300, the employee changes the amount to $500, cashes it at the second bank, deposits $300 at the first bank in the actual company account, then debits Cash for $300. Or the employee arranges with a dishonest vendor to accept a check for part of the payment due, then debits Cash and credits Accounts Receivable for the full amount due and splits the difference with the vendor.

Check Theft

There are three types of check theft:

1. **Stolen canceled checks or stolen check statements that contain images of the company's canceled checks.** The check thief opens an account in the company's name at a different bank, uses the stolen canceled check or bank statement check image to order checks from a mail-order check printer using the phony new company account, has them sent to a mail drop—then cashes the illicit checks using false identifications.

2. **Check washing.** This is widespread right now. The thief steals the checks from a mailroom or mailbox, covers every part of the check but the handwritten payee and amount and soaks it in a solution of chemicals available from any hardware store. When the payee and amount are dissolved, the thief writes in a new payee and amount and cashes the checks, usually for a small amount. These checks are generally accepted without question.

3. **Stolen check stock.** Professional thieves use sophisticated methods to steal blank check stock already encoded with customer account information, so that passing the check is easier. Corporate checks are the most likely target since they are easily cashed and deposited.

Other Check Fraud Schemes

Check kiting to cover fraud. This is one of the original white-collar crimes. Multiple bank accounts are opened, a "deposit" (the money never exists) is made in one account, then redeposited from one account to the next. The new bank credits the account before the old bank clears the check. Despite better ways to detect kiting, it still occurs because of *floating*, the practice of obtaining credit for deposited funds before the check clears the financial institution on which it is drawn. Your company is most susceptible to kiting if any one employee is authorized to write checks or make deposits in more than one bank account. While new technology keeps shortening the float, making it more difficult to kite, new laws make it easier by requiring banks to make funds from new deposits available before a check clears.

Paperhangers. Paperhangers are experts at passing phony checks. They pick an establishment or store and observe its security methods, generally bypassing those that appear to scrutinize a check writer's identification. When they choose an establishment, they select the least experienced or most lackadaisical employee to pass the check, ask if they may have cash back from the transaction, then make the check out for more than the purchase price. Variation: Making a fraudulent deposit at a bank and asking for cash back. This is harder to do if the business is a corporation.

Fraudsters go to great lengths to blend in with the clientele. Women are often good paperhangers—a mother with crying children paying with a check does not fit most people's image of a bad-check-passer.

Stop-payment orders. This scheme is simple. The "customer" purchases an expensive item with a check, then notifies his/her bank to stop payment. Savvy check passers may contact the merchant, saying the item was defective and that the merchant should expect to hear from the customer's attorney— meanwhile selling the item for a tidy profit. Variation: After purchasing the item and stopping payment, the fraudster returns the item to the store for a full refund in cash.

Forged travelers' checks. $100 travelers' checks are quite common, so some check rings specialize in producing and distributing them. Typically, these check passers make small purchases and receive the bulk of the $100 back in cash. Naturally, the scheme is most often used in areas that do a lot of tourist business, often several times in rapid succession.

Travelers' checks have several distinguishing features, including watermarks, holograms, microprinting, and ultraviolet ink. Counterfeits are generally produced in one of two ways:

1. **Color copying.** These counterfeits have a slick flat feel instead of the textured, raised-ink feel that the intaglio printing press gives to most real travelers' checks.

2. **Offset lithography/printing.** These counterfeits are higher quality than color-copied checks, but lack the texture and the watermarks, microprinting, or holograms of the genuine article.

Preventing—or Spotting— Forged Company Checks

Here are some ways to protect your company against check fraud.

1. **Take advantage of new technologies.** Company checks printed with the following techniques make forgery difficult or impossible:

   - "Prismatic lithography" creates a pattern of colors that are difficult to separate (separation is needed to reproduce them), even with special cameras, filters, and film.

   - Scrambled indicia printing appears to be a random pattern of tiny colored dots printed on the paper but when viewed though a colored filter, appears as a word or pattern.

- A "micro-line" printed on each check appears to the naked eye as a solid line, but under a magnifying glass is very small words or letters that are very difficult to recreate with the normal printing process. (Credit cards often use a micro-line.)

- A three-dimensional hologram is easily identifiable by the human eye, but impossible to reproduce using ordinary copiers or printers.

- A security seal on the back of the check that appears when held up to a light. Even skillful counterfeits do not have a seal.

2. **Know what to look for in canceled company checks.** Forgeries tend to be just different enough in color to stand out. To catch forged checks returned with the company bank statement, fan the checks. Even if no forgery is spotted, investigate any unusual gaps in check numbers. Also, investigate company checks outstanding for too long or too many checks with second endorsements.

Preventing Payroll-Related Check Fraud by Employees

Checks used to pay employment taxes are a favorite target for thieves because many are made out to a bank. Require that the owner, spouse, or outside bookkeeper review the endorsement on each payroll tax check every month.

If you use a payroll service, be aware that a dishonest check procurer who works for a payroll processing company may print duplicate payroll checks, which are sold to third parties. Employees at payroll services have access to personal information on the legitimate recipients of the payroll checks and may make use of that data in the future.

Other signs of fraud related to payroll include:

- ❑ Ghost employees on payroll, or phony overtime pay.
- ❑ A second endorsement on an employee's paycheck.
- ❑ A different endorsement on an employee's paycheck from the one you normally see.
- ❑ An employee not present when paychecks are delivered.
- ❑ No timecard for an employee.
- ❑ A timecard filled out in a supervisor's handwriting.
- ❑ A different looking signature on a timecard.
- ❑ Unemployment claims from someone on the payroll.
- ❑ An unexplained rise in salary expense or paid absences.

Preventing Check Fraud by Customers

Set up strict check acceptance procedures and a program to educate employees to recognize forged and fraudulent checks and check-passing schemes.

__Important:__ Do no attempt to implement any of the following controls without discussing them with the owner or management. If employees are told to examine a check for, say, three items (to see if the check is a forgery) and the business has a large number of customers, you may start to lose business. Or, employees will start to circle any three items on each check simply to get to the next customer. New customers may be insulted if an employee studies their check. Thus, it may be more practical to decide on one item on a check that you want employees to review and to have them call a supervisor for any other questionable items that the employee sees.

1. __Require the right identification to accept checks.__ For retailers, careful review of customer identification is the most important step in preventing check fraud. Consider the following elements for your company policy:

❑ Employees must require identification and make sure that the identification is valid: a valid driver's license or state identification signed by the customer and with a recent photograph—which may not be infallible because it is becoming easier to counterfeit driver's licenses, passports, and other identification. Never accept something as identification simply because it is small, laminated, rectangular, and has a picture. An employee who suspects a false i.d. should try to verify the address and phone number in a telephone book or with other information.

❑ Employees must ask for two photo i.d.s and cannot accept Social Security cards, business cards, birth certificates, library cards, organizational membership cards, unsigned credit cards, bank books, work permits, insurance cards, voter's registration cards, learner's permits, or letters.

❑ Employees must examine each piece of customer identification, even if they have seen so many hundreds of i.d.s that the process has become monotonous (check passers count on employees' eagerness to skip the business of examining i.d.s. precisely because it is boring).

Retailers should post their check-acceptance policy in plain view and try to use some kind of electronic security system. Either a prominently displayed policy or an electronic security system in plain view is a deterrent.

2. **Have a strict check acceptance policy that includes some or all of the following:**

❏ A dollar limit on a sale that can be accepted without a supervisor's approval (offers limited protection because most bad checks are for $25-$35 that tend to be examined less closely).

❏ A limit on the amount accepted by check based on average purchase price.

❏ Accepting checks for only the amount of the purchase (no cash back).

❏ Refuse post-dated checks.

❏ Require that checks be made out on the date of purchase.

❏ Insist that the check be signed in front of the employee and compare that signature with the one on the driver's license or state identification.

❏ Refuse checks from out-of-town banks; if impractical, require a photo I.D. and the customer's local and out-of-town address and phone number.

❏ Refuse second-party checks.

❏ Beware of individuals that make a substantial purchase with little regard for price.

❏ Always request approval for suspicious requests, such as a small order from a new customer followed by a huge order.

❏ Verification of certified checks, which can also be forged.

❏ Examination of travelers' checks to see if the endorsement on the check closely resembles the authorized signature (if it does not, the issuer may not redeem it; major travelers' check companies honor stolen travelers' checks only if the merchant unknowingly accepted them).

3. **Train employees to look for:**

❏ Signs of alterations or erasures, especially in the signature or numerical and written amounts.

❏ A check that does not have at least one perforated edge.

❏ The absence of any design in the background of check paper.

❏ The absence of either bank logo or the printing of the bank name in the regular lettering.

❏ The absence of the bank address on the check.

❏ A glossy, crayonish appearance or any lack of detail or sharpness (indicates counterfeiting).

❏ A smooth texture (a rough document may indicate that there have been erasures).

❏ Faded colors (may indicate chemical bleaching).

❏ Magnetic routing numbers (the numbers at the bottom of a check in computer-style type) properly printed in dull, nonreflective magnetic ink.

4. **Have employees ask for additional identification or consult a supervisor when:**

❑ A check has a number under 200.

❑ A check has digits added to the check number (fraudsters know that checks with a number under 200 are often scrutinized).

❑ The printing on the check does not seem uniform in texture or color, or slants up or down.

❑ The transit number in the top right corner does not match the electronically encoded number at the bottom of the check as they normally do on genuine checks.

❑ The check is not imprinted with the customer's name and address—the same address that is on the driver's license or other identification.

❑ The first three of the electronically encoded numbers (these indicate the state and district office of the issuer) do not match properly.

❑ The check number is not included in the encoded serial numbers at the bottom as it is on genuine checks.

❑ There is stamped information on the check.

❑ Numerical and written amounts do not agree.

❑ Presented with a check for a large amount by a new customer.

5. **Require employees to call a supervisor or at least scrutinize the check and identification of anyone who:**

❑ Is overly polite.

❑ Is especially nervous.

❑ Is aggressive.

❑ Acts hurried.

❑ Takes extreme caution and a lot of time to sign the check.

❑ Attempts to distract the employee while writing out a check.

Although the surest protection is refusing to accept checks, this may result in lost sales.

Systems That May Help to Prevent Check Fraud

Bank verification systems. Most banks have 900 numbers to call to find out if there are sufficient funds in the customer's account to cover the check, but they are expensive.

Shared information networks. These networks are used by banks and merchants to share information about fraudulent bank accounts and fraudulent check writers. The merchant enters the driver's license number of the person writing the check and/or the bank account number that the check is written on. The number is run against a central database of driver's license numbers and bank accounts that other merchants or banks have had problems with. If there is a match, the merchant is notified immediately.

Check guarantors. The merchant pays a small percentage of the amount of the check being guaranteed, such as 1.5%-2.25%. Thus, guaranteeing a customer's $100 check would cost the merchant between $1.50 and $2.25. Typically there is a monthly minimum, such as $25 a month. If the fees in a given month do not add up to $25, the merchant must still pay the guarantor $25 for that month. Some guarantors charge a "subscription fee"—a flat payment, such as $15 a month, in addition to the minimum. Guarantors may offer additional kinds of guarantees for an extra fee. For example, one guarantor covers the bank fees and interest on a returned check for an additional 11¢ per check and will cover checks on which a stop-payment order has been placed for an additional 2¢ per check.

QUIZ 1   CHECK FRAUD

Problem I.

Multiple choice. Circle the correct answer.

1. Check kiting involves . . .

   a. cashing a check on an account based on a deposit in that account that has not yet cleared the bank on which the deposit was drawn.
   b. cashing a check for an account that the check passer knows is closed.
   c. cashing a bad check for more than the amount of the purchase and getting cash back.
   d. cashing a check, then putting a stop-payment order on the check.

2. Paper hanging describes a practice that involves . . .

   a. cashing a bad check for more than the amount of the purchase and getting cash back.
   b. selecting the least experienced or most lackadaisical employee to pass a bad check.
   c. using women, preferably with crying children to pass a bad check.
   d. all of the above.

3. The most common denomination for a forged traveler's check tends to be . . .

   a. $10
   b. $100
   c. $50
   d. $25

4. Which of the following is a technique for spotting a forgery of your company's checks:

   a. Fanning company checks to spot a check whose color is slightly off
   b. Looking for checks that are outstanding for too long
   c. Looking for an excess number of checks with second endorsements
   d. All of the above

5. Which of the following should be investigated further to see if there is payroll-related fraud?

    a. A second endorsement on an employee's paycheck
    b. An unexpected rise in paid absences
    c. An employee not there when paychecks are delivered
    d. All of the above

6. For retailers, the *most important* step in preventing check fraud is making sure that employees . . .

    a. know how to spot forged checks.
    b. know how to spot counterfeit checks.
    c. accept only valid identification and examine each i.d., no matter how many checks they handle each day.
    d. tell customers about the company's check acceptance policy.

7. Which of the following should *not* be accepted as a valid form of identification for cashing a check?

    a. a driver's license
    b. a Social Security card
    c. a passport
    d. a signed credit card with a photograph of the customer

8. Which of the following may indicate that a customer's check is a forgery?

    a. Routing numbers on the bottom of the check are in shiny black ink.
    b. The check number is #187.
    c. The transit number in the top right corner does not match the electronically encoded number at the bottom of the check.
    d. All of the above.

Problem II.

Mark each question True or False.

1. A check that has no design in the background may indicate a forged check.

    a. True   b. False

2. If you run your fingers over a check and feel a rough texture where there is no writing, the check may be forged.

    a. True   b. False

3. Certified checks need not be verified because they cannot be forged.

    a. True   b. False

4. Prismatic lithography is a technique used in check printing to protect against forgery by creating a pattern of colors that are difficult to separate even with special cameras and filters.

    a. True   b. False

5. Check washing involves stealing checks from a company, dissolving the payee and amount with chemicals and writing in a new payee and amount.

    a. True   b. False

Problem III.

Fill in the blanks.

1. An employee should scrutinize the check and identification of any customer who acts _____ _____, _____ _____ , _____, or _____.

2. An employee should beware of individuals who take extra time and caution to complete the _____ on a check.

3. Employees should be suspicious of customers who attempt to _____ them while writing out a check.

4. To protect your company against having its checks forged, you can ask to have a _____ printed on each check, which appears to the naked eye as a solid line, but under a magnifying glass is very small words or letters.

5. One way to protect your company against having its checks forged is to have a three-dimensional _____ printed on them, because it is easily identifiable by the human eye, but impossible to reproduce using ordinary copying or printing.

QUIZ 1 Solutions and Explanations

Problem I.

   1. a
   2. d
   3. b
   4. d
   5. d
   6. c
   7. b
   8. d

Problem II.

   1. True
   2. True
   3. False
   4. True
   5. True

Problem III.

   1. overly polite, especially nervous, aggressive, hurried
   2. signature
   3. distract
   4. micro-line
   5. hologram

QUIZ 2   CHECK FRAUD

Problem I.

Multiple choice. Circle the correct answer.

1. "Scrambled indicia" are . . .

   a. a form of printing that appears to be a random pattern of tiny colored dots but when viewed through a colored filter shows a pattern of words.
   b. a technique used by forgers to create a false i.d.
   c. a technique used by forgers to recreate a company logo.
   d. a technique used by forgers to distract an employee from examining an i.d. or check.

2. A security seal is . . .

   a. a method of locking a cash box so that only the employee with the key can open it.
   b. a mark on the back of company checks that appears only when held up to a light.
   c. the mark that identifies a valid certified check.
   d. the stamp that an employee uses on a customer's check once it has been accepted.

3. Which of the following should never be accepted as identification from a customer who wants to pay by check?

   a. a birth certificate
   b. a membership card in a well-known local or national organization
   c. a bank book
   d. all of the above

4. A check guarantor . . .

   a. runs the check issuer's drive's license number or bank account number against a database of driver license numbers and bank accounts that other merchants or banks have had problems with.
   b. guarantees payment of a check in return for a percentage of the amount and a monthly fee.
   c. tells you if there are sufficient funds to cover a customer's check.
   d. is an electronic security system.

5. Checks used to pay employment taxes . . .

a. are a favorite of thieves because they are made out to a bank.
b. should have the endorsement checked by the owner, spouse, or bookkeeper on every one that the bank clears.
c. both a and b
d. neither a nor b

Problem II.

Mark each statement True or False.

1. One sign that a check may be a forgery is no perforated edge.

a. True   b. False

2. A small order from a new customer followed by a very large order should be carefully investigated.

a. True   b. False

3. On a genuine check, the transit number in the top right corner never matches the electronically encoded number at the bottom of the check.

a. True   b. False

Problem III.

Fill in the blanks.

1. In many states, when a check is written on insufficient funds, it is considered _____ _____ evidence that check fraud was intended.

2. When reviewing cancelled checks, it is a good idea to _____ them to spot a possible forged check.

3. When examining a customer's check, look for _____ colored paper, which may indicate chemical bleaching.

4. Beware of customers who make substantial purchases without regard for _____.

This page left blank intentionally.

QUIZ 2 Solutions and explanations

Problem I.

    1. a
    2. b
    3. d
    4. b
    5. c

Problem II.

    1. True.

    2. True

    3. False.
    On a genuine check, the transit number in the top right corner matches the electronically encoded number at the bottom of the check

Problem III.

    1. *prima facie*
    2. fan
    3. faded
    4. price

Introduction

Credit card fraud in the U.S. has reached nearly $1 billion, according to the National Fraud Information Center, 70% of which occurs during the holiday season when time is short and salespeople are hurried.

Credit card fraud works because the chances of being caught are small and prosecution is not assured. Among the laws covering credit card fraud is federal statute 15 U.S.C. 1644, which provides penalties of up to $10,000 and/or up to 10 years in prison for using counterfeit, fictitious, altered, forged, lost, stolen, or fraudulently obtained credit cards. But retailers report that when they identify credit card thieves to law enforcement, no action is taken.

At this writing, a lot of credit card fraud is committed by professional rings that steal credit cards, duplicate them, and express-mail them to ring members in other parts of the country. They also take bank information from the mail and use it to create driver's licenses, Social Security cards, and other false identification, which they use to make purchases with stolen cards. Spending sprees end only when the credit has dried up or the legitimate owner reports the card stolen.

Credit Card Fraud Prevention

The key to preventing fraud is making employees aware of how fraud schemes work as well as how to spot counterfeit or forged cards. If a significant part of your company's sales involve credit cards or your firm is particularly vulnerable to credit card fraud, your company should also develop strong liaison with law enforcement.

Establishing this liaison may take time and phone calls. Because local police are often not very concerned about financial crimes, you may have to call the district attorney's or sheriff's office or other regional law enforcement body. If you do not get an adequate response, you can call the nearest office of the FBI. Try to develop a relationship at the local level so that you know whom to contact if you do get a bad credit card—and hopefully they will alert you when bad cards hit your area. Any time you sense a lack of interest in credit card fraud, ask the law enforcement person whom they think is the best person or office for you to contact.

Schemes That Exploit
Lost or Stolen Cards

The following are common credit card fraud schemes. There is no need to memorize the schemes, but after reading about them, tips on how to detect forged or counterfeit credit cards will make more sense.

- **Fraudulent advance payments or overpayments.** Consumer laws require card issuers to credit customers' accounts *upon receipt of payment.* Fraud rings exploit these laws by using bad checks to reduce the amount owed on the credit cards they steal. Between the time that the thieves make their "advance payment" or "overpayment" with forged or counterfeit checks and the time when the card issuer discovers that the checks used to make the payments were bad, the rings have used the cards for numerous cash advances and purchases.

- **Shave and paste.** Any number of letters or numbers are sliced from the card surface, and different ones are attached to the card surface utilizing fast drying epoxy-type glues, resulting in an entirely different, but valid, account number or new name.

- **De-emboss/re-emboss.** The card is flattened to remove the embossed alpha-numeric characters. Plastic cards are made mostly of polyvinyl chloride, so they become more elastic when heated by a household iron, candle, hot water, or microwave oven. Fraudsters apply pressure to flatten the card, then use an embosser to create new numbers and names.

- **Counterfeit cards ("white plastic").** Fraudsters use a piece of plastic the size of a credit card that has account numbers and names embossed on it in collusion with a corrupt merchant or merchant's employee. Some organized crime groups operating in Taiwan, China, and Hong Kong, where the specialty is producing the holograms and magnetic strips that appear on many cards, use high-speed printers to manufacture credit cards from scratch. Forged holograms are smuggled into the U.S. and Canada by ring members from Asia and distributed throughout both countries. Many of them end up in California, where most of the Asian counterfeiting operations in the U.S. are located. Not surprisingly, California, notably Orange County, has more credit card fraud than any area in the country. Counterfeit credit cards cause the greatest losses.

Despite new technology in desktop computers, embossers, tipping foil, and laminators that allow for ever more accurate forgeries, duplicating legitimate cards is still an intricate operation. Magnetic strips, numbers, holograms, and logos must all appear authentic.

A phony hologram is still very difficult to produce, however, because the design is imbedded in the plastic. Thus, phony holograms can often be spotted by close inspection because they tend to be merely decals attached to the surface of the card. These phony holograms do not change color when viewed from different angles as legitimate ones do.

Getting victims' credit card numbers via phone or mail-order fraud. There are a variety of cons that induce victims to read their card numbers. For example, the victim may be asked for the card number as verification to get the discount deal being offered. A surprisingly large numbers of people readily cooperate. The thieves then make purchases from mail-order catalogs or flier sources using the address of a vacant house or apartment where they leave a note asking the deliverer to put the package by the back door.

Some typical schemes used to steal a victim's identity:

- That trip or other prize is free—as long as the victim verifies that he or she has a credit card by providing the card number and other data which the thieves use to order merchandise or have money wired to them.

- The thieves call random names from a phone book, pretend to be Visa or MasterCard representatives, claim that the victim's card number may have been obtained and used illegally by criminals, and request that the victim verify the card number by providing it.

- The thieves claim to be travel agency representatives, announce that the victim has won a discount travel package, and ask for his/her credit card number for verification.

Here are other ways that fraudsters use credit cards or the data on them to commit fraud:

- **False applications.** Perpetrators apply for a new card using information stolen from a wallet, purse, or the trash; steal a pre-approved credit card application from the mail or trash; or use "take-one" applications offering credit cards to the public that are available in many stores.

- **Credit "doctors."** These are fraudsters who sell stolen credit card account numbers to people unable to get credit cards. They simply put an ad in the paper.

- **True name fraud.** Any thief who has someone's driver's license or other i.d. can open new credit card accounts. The i.d.s are obtained in a robbery or by pick pocketing.

- **Nonreceipt fraud.** The fraudster intercepts valid credit cards sent by the issuer to the holder.

- **Merchant scams.** Sales people collude with the fraudster to get valid credit card numbers and print them on white plastic cards; or they make several imprints on sales tickets and fill them in later; or an employee uses a card left by a customer to make unauthorized purchases.

- **Skimmers.** These card-reading devices, similar to the swipe machine used by cashiers to validate credit cards, are becoming more prevalent. They can be purchased at electronic stores and used by credit card thieves to read data imprinted on information tracks in a credit card's magnetic strip. Criminals take the information from one credit card and put it on another.

- **Using merchant numbers.** After obtaining customers' carbon paper receipts, the fraudster watches a store employee dial the credit reporting agency to learn the numbers dialed, listens to the employee give the merchant number (or gets it from the paper taped on the cash register), calls the credit-reporting agency, and uses the merchant's number to verify that the card is valid and to find out how much credit is available.

How to Spot Credit Card Scams

1. **Unusual customer behavior.** While the following actions can occur in a legitimate transaction, they often signal attempted fraud. Tell employees to watch out for customers who:

   ❑ Take a card from a pocket instead of a wallet or purse.

   ❑ Purchase an unusual number of expensive items.

   ❑ Make random purchase with little regard for size, quality, or value.

   ❑ Make several small purchases under the floor limit or ask what the floor limit is.

   ❑ Sign the sales draft slowly or awkwardly.

   ❑ Charge expensive items on a newly valid credit card.

   ❑ Cannot provide photo identification when asked.

   ❑ Rush the merchant or teller.

   ❑ Purchase a large item, such as a television console, and insist on taking it at the time, even when delivery is included in the price.

   ❑ Become argumentative with the employee while waiting for the transaction to be completed.

Important: Do not attempt to require employees to use the following information without discussing it with the owner or management. If employees are told to examine a credit card for all of the following items to see if the card is a counterfeit, customers will be kept waiting and you may lose business, and new customers may be insulted if an employee studies their credit card. Thus, it may be more practical to decide on one item on a credit card that you want employees to review and to have them call a supervisor for any other questionable items that the employee sees.

2. **Signs of counterfeit cards.** *A* Money *magazine study found that 95% of* store clerks and cashiers do not check credit card signatures and cannot recognize counterfeit or forged cards. Keep in mind that counterfeiters may obtain the information on the magnetic strip on the back of the card, then create a plastic card that looks good enough to avoid calling employees' attention to it. Look for the following:

❑ A signature on the credit card that is inconsistent with the one on the charge-card slip—the key comparison to make on every transaction.

❑ A signature panel on the back of the card that is blank or damaged.

❑ Embossed characters that are not aligned or are not of the same size, height, and style.

❑ A hologram that is not distinct, not three dimensional, or does not give the illusion of moving when the card is tilted (imitation holograms are often easily damaged by scratching).

❑ A hologram that is crudely stamped or badly faked or has tiny bits of aluminum foil at the edges, indicating that it has been applied to the card (real holograms are stamped into the plastic, not stuck to the surface).

❑ Ghost images of numbers that appear behind the embossing on the front or back, indicating that the card has been re-embossed.

❑ A valid expiration date (tell employees never to accept an expired card).

❑ An expiration date that shows signs of tampering.

❑ Misspelled words.

❑ Discoloration.

❑ Items glued to the card.

❑ Anything painted on the card.

❑ White tape covering any part of the card.

❑ Any evidence that the card has been flattened (to permit restamping of the card with new numbers, a new expiration date, or other new data).

❑ Numbers on your firm's display that do not match the embossed numbers on the card when the card is swiped.

3. **Signs that a Visa or MasterCard is counterfeit.** Make sure that:

❑ The signature panel (white strip of adhesive with the card owner's signature) has "Visa" or "MasterCard" printed many times and is not plain white (indicates a counterfeit) or damaged (indicates an alteration).

❑ The numbers on the signature panel slant left and match the numbers on the front of the card.

❑ Under ultraviolet light, a large "MC" is visible on MasterCards, a large dove on Visa cards.

❑ The four-digit bank identification number (BIN) must be printed below and match exactly the first four digits of the embossed number or the card has been altered or is a counterfeit.

❑ Visa's embossed account numbers begin with a 4 and contain 13 or 16 digits, MasterCard's with a 5 and contain 16 digits.

❑ Microprinting is printing that appears to the naked eye to be a solid line, but under a magnifying glass is very small words or letters that are very difficult to recreate with normal printing.

4. **Signs that an American Express card is counterfeit.** Make sure that:

❑ The account number on the front should match the one on the back.

❑ The Centurion's head in the helmet should be printed with a high degree of clarity and detail similar to the heads portrayed on U.S. currency.

❑ The signature panel should have wavy black lines and should not be plain white (indicating a counterfeit card) or smudged (altered card).

❑ The card member account number should be 15 digits and should begin with 34 or 37.

❑ Under black light, the "AMEX" should appear and the Centurion should look phosphorescent.

Help from Credit Card Companies

Some issuers use *edits* that alert the system when a card that is generally used five times a month is suddenly used 25 times in one day.

Today, more issuers offer *smart cards* that contain a microprocessor memory chip, instead of holograms, to provide increased security.

Recommended Rules for Company Credit Cards

If your firm's employees use company credit cards:

- Make it clear that the cards are provided for employees' convenience *in conducting business*—no personal expenses can be charged unless specifically authorized by company policy.

- Personal expenses charged on the card must be promptly reimbursed to your company.

- Ask the employee to sign a waiver permitting the company to deduct from the employee's paycheck unsubstantiated business-related charges. (**Note:** Do not implement this policy without consulting an attorney about your state and local laws.)

- Pursue repayment of nonbusiness charges that the company pays on the employee's behalf.

- Insist on normal documentation for payment to vendors (the charge itself should not be accepted as documentation, only as proof that payment was made).

- Require that employees report theft or loss of the card within three days (even though most fraud occurs within hours of theft or loss) to avoid liability for fraudulent charges.

Preventing Online Company Credit Card Fraud

When making purchases

Card holders who are not physically present when making purchases are liable not only for the cost of the item, but also for a "chargeback" fee if they cancel the purchase. In other words, if employees make purchases online, the company may incur substantial fees if there is a problem with the item and the employee who charged it tells the company not to pay.

When selling online

Currently, the best prevention is fraud-detection software. Your Web designer can also help by keeping key applications separate and by installing firewalls on each server.

QUIZ 1   **CREDIT CARD FRAUD**

Problem I.

Multiple choice. Circle the correct answer.

1. If your company does substantial sales using credit cards, your company should develop a strong liaison with . . .

    a. credit card company security departments.
    b. law enforcement.
    c. bank credit card security departments.
    d. insurers that issue fidelity bonds.

2. Which of the following actions should lead employees to double-check a customer's identification and the credit card being used?

    a. The customer purchases an unusual number of items.
    b. The customer takes a credit card from a purse.
    c. The customer makes several small purchases that stay under the floor limit or asks what the floor limit is.
    d. The customer purchases a large item, such as a television console, and insists on having it delivered.

3. The first key step in checking a credit card is . . .

    a. examining the hologram to see if it is three-dimensional.
    b. checking the signature on the credit card against the one on the sales slip.
    c. checking the microline under a magnifying glass.
    d. looking for phosphorescence on the Centurion.

4. The embossed numbers on a credit card should . . .

    a. be of uniform height and style.
    b. be the same on the front and back of the card on an AMEX card.
    c. match the partial group of numbers on the signature panel of a Visa or MasterCard, which should also slant to the left.
    d. All of the above.

5. If your company gives employees company credit cards, it should require that employees report theft or loss of the card within _____ to avoid having the company held liable for fraudulent charges.

   a. 7 days
   b. 24 hours
   c. 3 days
   d. 48 hours

Problem II.

Fill in the blanks.

1. On a valid MasterCard, the signature panel has the word _____ printed numerous times.

2. On a valid Visa card, the signature panel has the word _____ printed numerous times.

3. On a valid Visa or MasterCard, the four-digit BIN, which stands for _____ _____ _____, must be printed below and match exactly the first four digits of the embossed number.

4. Visa card account numbers begin with the numeral ___ and contain ___ or ____ digits.

5. MasterCard embossed account numbers begin with the numeral ___ and contain ___ digits.

6. American Express account numbers begin with the numerals ___ or ___ and contain ___ digits.

7. Microprinting should be near the logo on all _____ credit cards.

QUIZ 1 Solutions and explanations

Problem I.

    1. b
    2. c
    3. b
    4. d
    5. c

Problem II.

    1. MasterCard
    2. Visa
    3. bank identification number
    4. 4, 13, 16
    5. 5, 16
    6. 34, 37, 15
    7. Visa

QUIZ 2   **CREDIT CARD FRAUD**

Problem I.

Multiple choice. Circle the correct answer.

1. On a valid American Express card, the signature panels should have . . .

    a. the words "American Express" repeated numerous times.
    b. the word "AMEX" repeated numerous times.
    c. wavy black lines .
    d. nothing on the white adhesive tape.

2. To minimize losses from employee misuse of company credit cards, a company should . . .

    a. make it company policy to deduct from an employee's paycheck any personal or unsubstantiated business charges owed.
    b. have employees sign a waiver permitting the company to deduct from the employee's paycheck any personal or unsubstantiated business charges not repaid by an employee.
    c. consult a lawyer about having employees sign a waiver permitting the company to deduct from an employee's paycheck any personal or unsubstantiated business charges not repaid by an employee.
    d. use a, b or c depending on the company's management style.

3. To minimize losses from employee misuse of credit cards, a company . . .

    a. should insist on normal documentation for payments to vendors made on the cards.
    b. can use the credit card statement as documentation for payments to vendors on the cards.
    c. should not permit employees to pay vendors with company-provided cards.
    d. should offer employees the option of using normal documentation for payments to vendors made on the cards.

4. An employer that permits employees to make purchases online with a company credit card should anticipate that if the employee is dissatisfied with the product and refuses to pay the bill, the company is very likely . . .

    a. to be sued by the credit card company.
    b. to be sued by the vendor.
    c. to pay a substantial chargeback fee.
    d. to be prosecuted for violation of federal statute 15 U.S.C. 1644.

5. Which of the following should alert an employee to possible credit card fraud and induce the employee to either ask for additional identification or seek a supervisor's help?

    a. A customer who makes random purchases with little regard to size, quality, or value.
    b. A customer who charges expensive items on a newly validated card.
    c. A customer who takes a charge card from a pocket instead of from a wallet or purse.
    d. All of the above.

Problem II.

Fill in the blanks.

1. A valid Visa credit card's embossed number contains either _____ or _____ digits and begins with the numeral ____.

2. A MasterCard's embossed number contains ____ digits and begins with the numeral _____.

3. An American Express card's embossed number should be ___ digits in length and begin with the numerals ____ or ____.

4. When you put an American Express card under a black light, the word ____ should appear and the_____ should look phosphorescent.

5. The key first step in preventing credit card fraud is to check the _____ on the credit card against the _____ on the sales slip.

6. It is extremely inadvisable to ever accept a(n) _____ credit card.

This page left blank intentionally.

QUIZ 2 Solutions and explanations

Problem I.

1. c
2. c
3. a
4. c
5. d

Problem II.

1. 13, 16, 4
2. 16, 5
3. 15, 34, 37
4. AMEX, Centurion
5. signature, signature
6. expired

Section 5
HOW VENDORS CHEAT YOU

Bribery

The earliest definitions of *bribery* were based on corruption of government officials and included offering, giving, receiving, or soliciting anything of value to influence an *official act* of government. Simply *offering* payment to influence a decision constituted a bribe, even if no payment was made. It was the *expectation* of payment that defined bribery.

In *commercial bribery*, something of value is offered to influence a business decision. What distinguishes bribery from legal and ethical payments to win contracts or bids is that the purchasing organization's employee receives the payment in return for using his/her influence *without his/her employer's consent*. In other words, the company is *not* aware that the employee is influencing a business decision in return for under-the-table payments.

Employees acting as agents for their employer owe that employer a duty of loyalty and are legally required to act in the employer's best interests and to refrain from self-dealing or using their position to further personal interests at the employer's expense. Accepting something of value to influence or base a business decision on one's own best interests instead of on the employer's best interests violates the duty of loyalty.

Forms of Bribery

Bribery is generally off the books and takes various forms, including gifts, loans, payment of credit card bills and kickbacks. Because bookkeepers are rarely in a position to detect bribery, it is not covered in depth here. For a description of bribery schemes, see Appendix A, Forms, Patterns and Red Flags of Bribery,

Telemarketing Frauds

Although most telemarketing frauds are aimed at consumers, some target businesses. Telemarketing scams are easy to set up because they require little more than a hit-and-run phone room, can operate in a different state hundreds of miles from the victims, are rarely reported, and are supported by a web of legitimate businesses that make money supplying the fraudsters. (See Appendix B, Operations That Support Frauds and Scams.) The 1 in 100 victims who files a complaint with law enforcement discovers that few resources are devoted to the prosecution of such acts.

Telemarketing Scams That
Target Businesses

Telemarketing frauds range from basic to complex. Many of the most popular scams are aimed at the business owner. Some of the more common scams targeting businesses including the following:

Advertising materials scams

<u>The scam</u>: Companies constantly seek new ways to advertise. Fraudulent telemarketers take advantage of this by calling and offering to advertise the company on note pads, calendars, and other materials to be distributed in the nearby area. They require an upfront fee—but never produce or distribute anything.

Your company can protect itself by taking the following steps:

❑ Before buying, get references (previous buyers) and samples of produced materials.

❑ Don't be pressured into agreeing to anything immediately.

❑ Compare the prices and quality offered to those of local vendors. This is particularly important when making purchases for items you have never dealt with before. For example, if you are a bookkeeper and are offered a "special deal" on advertising materials, you may think they are cheap—until you compare the prices with those of local vendors.

❑ If you never heard of the business, ask the Better Business Bureau or local consumer protection office if there have been complaints about it. A lack of complaints does not assure legitimacy, but the presence of complaints may be an important factor in your decision.

❑ Get a written contract.

❑ If you are required to make a down payment, make it as small as possible and retain the balance until your company approves the materials and you have checked out the company.

Internet services scams

<u>The scam:</u> Telemarketers contact businesses and offer to set up a Website, create banner ads, list the company in a directory or Internet mall, or provide other Internet services to the business. Once payment is received, no services are performed.

Your company can protect itself by taking the following steps:

❑ Shop around for Internet access, Website designers, and other Internet services. Start by asking other companies for referrals: look in the phone book or online.

❑ Decide whether you want a vendor in your geographical area.

❑ Look at samples of previous work.

❑ Be suspicious of offers for Internet services that are incredibly cheap.

❑ Find out all the terms of "special offers" and "free trial periods."

Paper and Toner Scams

<u>The scam</u>: If your firm uses a particular office supply company, fraudulent telemarketers will take advantage of this by calling, claiming to be from your regular supplier, and offering a great deal on copier paper, toner cartridges, and other supplies. They will ask that you pay when the supplies—generally inferior and overpriced—are dropped off.

To protect your firm . . .

❑ tell employees to be skeptical of callers claiming to be from your regular office supplier with a "last chance" offer to buy supplies before prices go up;

❑ tell employees to ask for the person's name, company name and phone number—preferably a switchboard number (although some legitimate firms may no longer have a switchboard number);

❑ do not pay invoices for supplies without checking that your company has received them;

❑ have a designated employee in charge of ordering office supplies—an employee who knows about office supplies is much harder to dupe; and

❑ dispute *in writing* a bill for supplies that are unsatisfactory or that were misrepresented (but this may not help if the sale is a scam).

Loan scams

<u>The scam</u>: Calls offering your firm an unsecured loan "even if you have credit problems"—if you pay a fee in advance. The loan never materializes.

Your company can protect itself by taking the following steps:

❑ If your firm needs a loan, first ask your firm's bank, which is likeliest to make the loan because it knows your firm's reputation. Only if your firm's bank refuses the loan should you consider sources of loans unfamiliar to your company's owners.

❑ If your firm's bank turns down a request for a loan, ask if there is anything that can be done to reverse the decision, such as putting up collateral or getting a co-signer.

❑ Do not believe ads that promise loans regardless of past credit problems.

❑ Be cautious of unsolicited calls, e-mails, or letters that offer your company a loan.

❑ Red flags: upfront "processing," "application," or "first-month payment" fees.

❑ Get all loan terms in writing, including payment schedule and interest rate, before signing.

If your firm has ever been scammed, expect that it will be "reloaded" or contacted again by the original scammer soliciting additional payments.

Buyers Clubs Scams

The scam: To take advantage of businesses seeking to save money by joining buyers clubs offering products in bulk, fraudulent telemarketers sign you up for clubs that do not exist.

Your firm can protect itself by telling employees to . . .

❑ be wary of offers at very low prices or free products that require payment only for shipping;

❑ be aware that, just because a marketer has the company's financial information, this does not mean that it is a legitimate vendor;

❑ ask for details before joining;

❑ comparison-shop for the best deals;

❑ ask for clarification, possibly in writing, of a "trial offer";

❑ be leery of "welcome packages" where you are asked to pay "only shipping and handling"; and

❑ contact the credit card issuer or bank immediately for unauthorized charges or debits on the company account by a "buyers club."

Telemarketing scams enforcement

As the number and strength of the illegal operations have risen, so have enforcement efforts. In 1995, the Federal Trade Commission won new laws to curb telemarketing fraud. Because honest vendors know about the law and comply with it, one way to tell if a vendor is honest is to note whether it complies with the new laws' requirements that:

- salespeople clearly identify themselves and their enterprise, including a phone number at which they can be reached;

- the vendor provide certain services and information before demanding payment;

- the vendor can call only between 8 a.m. and 9 p.m.; and

- the details of the offer be clearly stated or written and easy to understand ("clear and conspicuous") *before the sale is closed*. Thus, your company's employee should have no problem understanding the terms of the sale and no problem obtaining a written explanation in a pdf, by fax, or in the mail.

Resources for Protecting Your Company

If you have concerns about a vendor's legitimacy, you can contact the following:

Federal Bureau of Investigation (FBI). Lists "Common Fraud Scams" and their warning signs at www.fbi.gov/majcases/fraud/fraudschemes.htm.

Better Business Bureau (BBB). Its Web page, search.bbb.org/results.html, tells you if a company has complaints against it including but not limited to fraud, and provides details on whether the complaints were resolved. Although the BBB will not tell you *how* they were resolved, the volume of complaints should be a good indicator.

National Fraud Information Center (NFIC). Tracks telemarketing, Internet and other frauds and ranks them by frequency at www.fraud.org/welcome.htm.

Federal Trade Commission (FTC). Consumer Response Center. Phone toll-free 1-877-382-4357. www.ftc.gov.

Prosecution of Fraudulent Telemarketers

Telemarketing boiler rooms are usually run by veteran criminals who know how to set up and shut down operations quickly. Prosecution is difficult because they can start up with little more than a warehouse, tables, a script, and some phones. By the time enough complaints are generated to initiate an investigation, its participants have packed up and left.

Many states have laws that require telephone sales companies to register with the Attorney General's office and, in some cases, demand a cash bond to cover potential losses. But there is little enforcement of registration and, when companies register, little verification of the information. Telemarketers avoid trade laws and scrutiny by local law enforcement by not calling anyone in the state in which they operate. Many set up in foreign countries, often former members of the Soviet Union, and target U.S. consumers.

Most legal actions against the fraudsters are civil (not criminal) suits that are settled with a judgment for damages that are uncollectible and a consent decree (a promise not to violate certain laws and to refrain from operating an illegal business in the future) that is rarely honored. Such minor judgments encourage offenders to go from one operation to the other, treating fines and settlements as a cost of business. Although prosecutions involving prison sentences have risen, the best protection for a company is still prevention.

QUIZ 1   HOW VENDORS CHEAT YOU

Problem I.

Multiple choice. Circle the correct answer.

1. What distinguishes bribery from legal and ethical payments to win contracts is that the purchasing organization's employee . . .

   a. uses personal influence to help the vendor get the contract.
   b. receives payment.
   c. receives payment in return for using personal influence.
   d. receives payment in return for using personal influence without the employer's consent.

2. Employees acting as agents for their employer are *legally* required to . . .

   a. report co-workers who break company rules.
   b. act in the employer's best interests when making business decisions.
   c. act in a businesslike way when conducting company business.
   d. do their job to the best of their ability.

3. If your company receives a call offering a special deal on advertising materials, the employee should not agree to buy anything before:

   a. getting references and samples of produced materials
   b. checking the company's name with the Better Business Bureau
   c. comparing prices with those of local vendors.
   d. All of the above

4. Which of the following are important when responding to Internet services offered by a telemarketer?

   a. Get all the terms on free trial periods of other special offers.
   b. Be leery of welcome packages.
   c. Consider a first-month payment fee a red flag.
   d. all of the above.

5. Which of the following steps should you take before moving forward with a loan offered to your company by a telemarketer?

   a. Ask your company's bank and, if it refuses, consider other sources.
   b. Ask your company's bank and if it refuses ask if your firm can do anything to reverse the bank's decision.
   c. Assume that it is a scam if the loan is promised regardless of past credit problems.
   d. All of the above.

6. Which of the following is a way to prevent buying paper or toner from a telemarketing fraudster?

   a. Ask for samples before buying.
   b. Have a designated employee in charge of ordering office supplies.
   c. Dispute any bills that are inaccurate.
   d. All of the above.

7. Which of the following is an indication that a telemarketing offer for a buyer's club may be on the level?

   a. The prices are good and shipping is free.
   b. The caller already has your company's financial data.
   c. The caller offers to fax details of the offer by fax before you sign.
   d. The vendor offers low prices and free shipping.

Problem II. Fill in the blanks.

1. Under current federal law, salespeople who call you must clearly identify _____ and their _____, including a _____ _____ at which they can be reached; must provide certain _____ and _____ before demanding payment; can call only between ___ a.m. and ___ p.m., and must make the details of the offer _____ and _____ before the sale is closed.

2. One place to keep up on current fraud scams is the FBI's _____ _____ _____ Web page.

This page left blank intentionally.

QUIZ 1 *Solutions and explanations*

Problem I.
1. d
2. b
3. d
4. a
5. b
6. b
7. c

Problem II.
1. themselves, enterprise, phone number, services, information; 8, 9; clear, conspicuous
2. Common Fraud Scams

QUIZ 2   HOW VENDORS CHEAT YOU

Problem I.

Multiple choice. Circle the correct answer.

1. The best place to check out a vendor for complaints not only about fraud but about other problems as well is:

   a. the FBI
   b. the BBB
   c. the NFIC
   d. the FTC

2. One indication that a telemarketing offer may be fraudulent would be that . . .

   a. the salesperson does not clearly identify him- or herself and the enterprise.
   b. the salesperson demands payment before providing any services or products.
   c. the details of the offer are neither clearly stated nor clearly written.
   d. all of the above.

3. Accepting something of value to influence a business decision on one's own interests instead of on the employer's interests violates . . .

   a. business ethics.
   b. the duty of loyalty.
   c. the obligation to tell the truth.
   d. the expectation of remuneration.

4. Commercial bribery has taken place when an employee has influenced a business decision without the employer's knowledge . . .

   a. after receiving a gift
   b. after a weekend away at a vendor's expense
   c. in expectation of payment for doing so
   d. in return for a vendor paying the employee's credit card bill

Problem II.

Fill in the blanks.

1. If your company accepts a telemarketer's offer for-low cost advertising materials, it should compare the telemarketing company's _____ and _____ to those of _____ _____.

2. If your company accepts a telemarketer's offer for low-cost Internet services, it should be wary of offers that are very _____ and get all terms on _____ _____ _____ or other _____ _____.

3. If your company does not have a designated employee in charge of office supplies and decides to purchase paper or toner from a telemarketer, it should not pay for supplies until verifying that your company has _____ them; and if any supplies are unsatisfactory or have been misrepresented, it should dispute the bill _____ _____.

4. The first place to go before accepting a telemarketer's offer of a business loan is to your company's _____.

5. If your company is telemarketed by a buyer's club, it should be wary of offers at very low prices or free products that require payment only for _____.

QUIZ 2 Solutions and explanations

Problem I.

1. b
2. d
3. b
4. c

Problem II.

1. products, prices, local vendors
2. cheap, free trial periods, special offers
3. received, in writing
4. bank
5. shipping

This page left blank intentionally.

Forms, Patterns, and Red Flags of Bribery

Forms of Bribery

Illegal gratuities

Illegal gratuities—gifts or payments given after a decision is made and therefore with no apparent intent to influence it—are nevertheless a crime because they involve offering and accepting a gift, regardless of motive. For example, BuyCo awards a multimillion dollar contract to SellCo, based largely on BuyCo employee Green, who made a fair, open decision. Two weeks later, the SellCo CEO arranges and pays for a vacation for Green's family. This is an illegal gratuity because it is based on Green's decision, regardless of whether the gratuity influenced Green's decision.

Loans

Three types of "loans" often turn up in fraud cases:

1. a loan made on favorable terms or interest-free;

2. a loan that is actually a payment disguised as a loan; and

3. a loan on which the briber or briber's agent either makes the payments or guarantees the payments.

Payment of credit card bills

The briber pays the employee's credit card bill, which may include vacation or entertainment, expenses, or lets the employee use the briber's credit card.

Transfers of property at below-market value

The briber sells or leases property to the corrupt employee at far less than its market value or agrees to buy or rent property at inflated prices. Or the corrupt employee "sells" an asset to the briber but retains title or use of it.

Promises of favorable treatment

These include promises to:

☐ a government official of lucrative employment when the official leaves government service;

☐ an executive of favorable or inflated retirement and separation benefits when the person leaves a private firm for a related government position;

☐ the targeted employee's relative of an inflated salary or a "straw" job.

Kickbacks and overbilling

A *kickback*, in the commercial sense, is something of value received by a corrupt employee to influence a business decision without the employer's knowledge. Generally employees in purchasing who have both direct contact with vendors and the authority to approve payment of fraudulent invoices are the targets.

However, even employees who lack the authority to approve payment can receive kickbacks by forging purchase orders, support documentation, or signatures. In many companies, controls are so lax that even employees with no authority for purchasing can successfully recommend the purchase of fraudulently priced goods or services.

Overbilling. Once bribers obtain a contract, they give the corrupt employee a kickback to make sure that their inflated or fraudulent invoices (which include the cost of the kickbacks) are paid. Because the corrupt vendors no longer have to compete, they charge higher prices and keep the deal going by threatening to expose the employee. Thus, bribery schemes become quicksand for corrupt employees.

The key to a bribery scheme is the capacity of participating employees to rationalize their dishonest acts. At first they tell themselves that the vendor wants only what any company wants—a little extra business. Their employer is not being overcharged, so no one is hurt. This is completely false because accepting gifts in return for diverting business *is a crime*, regardless of the cost to the employer. Moreover, the employer always ends up paying more.

Once the scheme is underway, the size and nature of the payments are generally transformed from a small diversion of business into a major overbilling scheme. The more that corrupt employees try to help the corrupt vendor in order to get off the hook, the more deeply involved they become.

Patterns of Bribery

Bribery, like most business fraud, tends to last for extended periods. The following pattern is typical, but any of the steps can occur at any time.

Step #1. Small gifts, travel, and entertainment. Relatively small gifts and favors are offered not so much as inducements for a contract or piece of business, as to ingratiate the briber, create a relationship, and develop a level of influence on the employee's decisions.

Typical gifts or favors include:

☐ consumables, such as wine and liquor;

☐ clothes and jewelry for the recipient or spouse;

☐ lavish entertainment;

☐ paid vacations;

☐ free transportation on corporate jets;

☐ free use of resort facilities;

☐ sexual favors; and

☐ gifts of inventory or services, such as construction of home improvements by a contractor.

Step #2: Cash payments. At some point, the bribery advances to cash payments, which are difficult to trace. But large sums are not practical because they are hard to come up with and, under current law, draw attention when deposited or spent. The IRS now requires virtually any entity that receives $10,000 or more in cash to report that cash on a specific form.

Step #3: Checks and other financial instruments. Illicit payments in the form of a business check, cashier's check, or wire transfer are made directly or through an intermediary and disguised on the payer's books as some sort of business expense, typically consulting fees.

Step #4: Hidden interests. In the later stages of sophisticated schemes, the payer might provide the recipient with a hidden interest in a joint venture or other profit-making enterprise and conceal it in a straw business entity, hide it in a trust, or simply make an oral agreement. These deals are difficult to detect. Even when they are uncovered, proving corruption may be difficult.

Bid rigging

In competitive bidding, vendors vie for contracts on an equal footing, offering bids under the same terms and conditions as competitors, based on the purchaser's specs. Each vendor submits a confidential bid stating the price at which they will complete a project in accordance with the specs. Although the process is structured to be fair, it is tailor-made for bribery because any advantage can mean huge profits. A little inside influence can win a contract, so corrupt bidders try to rig bids by bribing a purchasing organization's employee. Sooner or later the purchasing organization pays the cost of the bribe through a higher contract price.

How a bid is rigged depends on the corrupt employee's level of influence. Favorite targets are buyers, contracting officials, engineers and technical representatives, quality or product assurance representatives, subcontractor liaison employees, and others with authority over the awarding of contracts. Bid-rigging schemes can occur at any of the three phases of the bidding process: pre-solicitation, solicitation, and submission.

Phase 1: Pre-solicitation. During the period before bids are officially sought, *need recognition schemes* and *specification schemes* are used.

Need recognition schemes. Purchasing organization Lee is paid to convince her firm that a particular project is needed, so her firm buys unneeded goods or services from the supplier at her direction. Typical signs of need recognition fraud include unusual needs, such as:

- unusually high requirements for stock and inventory;
- unusually large amounts of inventory being written off as scrap;
- "needs" that can be met only by a certain supplier or contractor; or
- failure to develop a satisfactory list of backup suppliers (leading to an unusually strong attachment to a primary supplier).

Specification schemes. The vendor pays the corrupt employee to:

- draft the contract specs to accommodate its capabilities; or
- classify the project as "sole-source," eliminating competitive bidding; or
- write vague specs that require amendment at a later date when the supplier can raise its price based on the new specs; or
- split a big project into several small ones that fall below the mandatory bid level so that the briber is guaranteed some or all parts of the contract (referred to as *bid splitting*).

Each scheme results in the purchasing firm paying more than it should pay.

Phase 2: Solicitation. Three kinds of schemes prevent the purchasing company from getting the best price: *bid pooling, fictitious suppliers*, and *destruction of legitimate bids*.

1. **Bid pooling.** Bidders conspire to make sure that each gets at least one job. Vendor A's bid will be the lowest bid on Contract #1, Vendor B's the lowest bid on Contract #2, and Vendor C's the lowest bid on Contract #3. None gets all three jobs, but each is assured one—and at a higher price than it would have gotten with competitive bidding.

2. **Fictitious** suppliers are created to make high bids so that the conspiring supplier is assured the job—most likely at inflated prices that are lower than those of its nonexistent competitors.

3. **Destruction of legitimate bids.** Legitimate bids are accepted but are "lost" or improperly disqualified by a corrupt employee, guaranteeing the contract to the favored vendor.

Phase 3: Submission. Several schemes may be used to win the contract for a supplier.

Competitive bids are confidential and should remain sealed until a specified date when all bids are opened and reviewed by the purchasing company. A corrupt vendor may bribe an employee to see its competitors' bids before submitting its bid to know just what price to submit to win the job, to extend the date on which the company will open the bids, or to control the way in which the bids are opened.

Red Flags of Bribery

Most bribery schemes are detected through tips from honest or disgruntled coworkers or vendors. Larger companies should establish and publicize systems to encourage and facilitate such reports, including confidential hotlines and contractor disclosure programs, and should create whistleblower protection policies.

Red flags in the bidding process that also corroborate illegal conduct:

❏ A pattern of contract awards to other than the lowest qualified bidder

❏ Unusual bidding patterns, such as:
- winning bids, or all bids, that are too high
- losing bidders appear as subcontractors
- predictable rotation of winning bidders on a geographical or other basis
- the same address, calculations, or errors on two or more bids
- the same or similar bids each time the same job is offered for bids
- few bidders or the same bidders keep showing up
- prices drop when a new bidder enters competition

❏ The apparent leaking of competitor's bids or other confidential information to a particular bidder, which may be indicated by:
- the last bidder always winning

- the contracting official extending the bid date after some bids are received or accepting late bids
- alterations to a bid
- a winning bid price coming in just under the next lowest bid
- contracts re-bid after the first round

❑ Large, unexplained differences in bid prices between bidders, which may be a sign of:

- collusive bidding, which is generally revealed when a new or honest bidder offers substantially lower prices than previous bidders who may be part of a bid-rigging cartel
- unbalanced bidding, which may signal that an insider has tipped off a favored bidder that certain items in the bid specs will not be needed, allowing "low-ball" bids on these items
- change-order abuse, a sign that the low bidder may have inside connections or is involved in a scheme to increase the price of the work after the bid has been accepted

❑ Fewer bidders than expected, or awards of contracts without the minimum number of bids

❑ Qualified contractors don't bid (may indicate rigged specs, bidding manipulation, collusive bidding, or corruption)

❑ Unknown bidders (may indicate a shell company used in a bid-rigging scheme)

❑ Low-bid award followed by significantly increased payments to the contractor

❑ Excessive, expensive, or undocumented change orders; repeated questionable change orders by certain contractors approved by the same contracting employee

❑ Sole-source awards in violation of procurement rules or standard procedures, particularly when the same supplier gets repeated awards in noncompetitive procurements

❑ Unreasonably narrow contract specs that appear to assure selection of a favored contractor

Red flags of employee corruption—or vulnerability to corruption

❑ Purchasing employees who accept inappropriate gifts, travel, or entertainment

❑ Employees with procurement responsibilities living beyond their apparent means

❑ Sudden, unexplained wealth displayed by an employee with purchasing responsibilities

❑ Employees who make accelerated payments on mortgages or on auto or consumer debt.

❑ Employees suddenly have extreme financial problems

❑ Employees who show signs of extreme stress or emotional disturbance.

❑ Employees who are unhappy about compensation, promotions, working conditions, or lack of appreciation by superiors

❑ Employees in purchasing who assume responsibilities above or below their normal duties, especially when they are involved in unusual actions with a particular vendor.

❑ Employees who fail to accept an apparently desirable promotion from a purchasing or contracting position (may indicate kickbacks or a hidden interest in a supplier).

❑ Employees who refuse to take vacation or time off or work excessive hours over an extended period coupled with other fraud indicators.

❑ High turnover in the contract or procurement department (honest employees often quit or transfer if they suspect wrongdoing, particularly if they lack secure means to report it)

❑ Deliberate or repeated failure to enforce existing controls and purchasing procedures—such as competitive bidding—or proper documentation of payment requests

❑ Insistence that contractors use a certain subcontractor, agent, middleman, or broker

❑ Unusually keen interest in certain transactions, contractors, or accounts or assuming responsibility for matters beyond the normal scope of the employee's duties

❑ Repeated, unjustified or unexplained favorable treatment of a contractor or supplier.

❑ Frequent excuses for deficiencies in a vendor's poor quality, late deliveries, or high prices.

❑ Close socializing with contractors, especially if accompanied by other fraud indicators

Red flags of vendor attempts at corruption

❑ A salesperson or contractor who routinely offers inappropriate gifts, provides lavish business entertainment, or tries to ingratiate him-/herself through unethical means

❑ Continual contracts to a supplier that provided unsatisfactory goods, services, or prices.

❑ Persistent allegations or rumors of wrongdoing by an employee or vendor.

❑ Repeated discrepancies or "errors" by a contractor in submitted data, test results, or invoices

❑ Discrepancies or errors in proposed v. actual costs, or claimed costs v. support documents

❑ Consistent poor quality of service or product, late deliveries or other persistent deficiencies

Other red flags

❑ Unusual or unjustified high prices or extreme price increases

❑ Discrepancies between prices quoted and charged in a cost-type contract

❑ Expenses that significantly overrun budget projections.

❑ Departments or employees who are consistently over budget

❑ Purchase prices out of line with market rates

❑ Multiple payments to the same supplier in the same or similar amounts

❑ Multiple awards just under the competitive bidding or upper-level review limits.

❑ Purchases of goods or services in excessive amounts

❑ Purchases of unneeded or inappropriate goods or services

❑ Unjustifiably high volume of purchases made from a supplier or contractor

❑ Excess purchases from a particular vendor or deviation from a standard vendor rotation

❑ Payment for goods or services without confirmation of receipt.

❑ Purchases without required purchase orders (may indicate attempts to evade purchase review)

❑ Notations on invoices for "extra" or "special" charges

❑ Missing inventory or the inability to account for invoiced goods or services

❑ Apparently inflated labor or material charges; missing, altered, or out-of-date supporting documents; or the failure to pass on discounts or rebates received by the vendor

Keeping Suppliers Honest

The best method of preventing vendor fraud is to check out the vendors you are considering doing business with before you sign the contract.

Conduct background checks

Check public records, online subscription services, such as Dun & Bradstreet, and the Internet (see page 63) for general background information on the vendor. Particularly note the vendor's:

❑ ownership;

❑ affiliates;

❑ customers;

❑ sales volumes;

❑ whether the contractor is a sales rep firm (a broker or middleman) or manufacturer; and

❑ litigation history.

Check their references

Before doing business with a new vendor, ask for a list of other customers. Chances are you may know one or more businesses on the list. Call them for their opinion. If you don't know anyone on the list or are suspicious of any of the names, ask for more names and do further checking.

Check their bills and invoices

Make sure you follow the advice offered in this manual, particularly to have someone independently review invoices before they are paid. The person procuring the services should not be the person issuing payment. Also, if an invoice is not initialed by an employee, don't pay it until you find out whether the services were performed or the goods received.

Question your company's suppliers

Vendors know that many people do not question bills for fear of offending the supplier, so many vendors inflate bills. If anything looks out of order, *call.* You have a right to question bills before paying them. Calling lets vendors know their bills are reviewed before payment. This inhibits bill padding.

Use vendor questionnaires

Another useful tool is to ask vendors to complete a vendor questionnaire. Often, the information on the questionnaire can help identify problems before they occur. Also, if you continue to have a relationship with a particular vendor, send out annual questionnaires to ensure that the information you have is current.

<u>Important</u>: The following questionnaire should be used only as a general model. Questions should be deleted, added, or modified based your company's industry, relationships with its vendors and the checks and balances that it normally applies to vendors before doing business with them.

Vendor Questionnaire

1. How long has your company been in business? _____

2. How long have you done business with our company? _____

3. Approximately what percentage of your total business does our company represent? _____

4. How many employees do you have in your organization? _____

a. Do any of our former employees work for you or are any of your employees related to any of our employees? If yes, what are their names and titles?
_____

5. Which personnel in your company are responsible for soliciting business from us?
_____

6. Whom do you contact in our company? _____

7. In the course of doing business with us, have you encountered any difficulties? If so, what could our company have done differently to help rectify the problem(s)?
_____

_____

8. Are you aware of our company's Standards of Business Conduct Policy? _____

9. a. Does your company own or rent any of the following:

    __ Hunting camp   __ Recreation retreat   __ Airplane   __ Tennis club
    __ Fishing camp   __ Motor home   __ Golf course membership   __ Pleasure boat

    b. Is there a guest log? _____ May we see it? _____

10. Which of our employees have utilized any of these? How often? Over what time period?
_____

11. Does your company sponsor:

    __ Christmas parties   __ Golf outings   __ Picnics   __ Fishing trips   __ Other events

12. Does your company provide annual or periodic gifts? _____ What is their dollar value? _____
    To whom? _____

13. Does your company provide any other gratuities to our employees? _____
    To whom? _____

14. Does your company make any payments to any of our employees or their relatives? _____
    To whom? _____

15. Does your company make any payments to companies in which one of our employees has an interest? _____ What are their names _____

Appendix B
Operations That Support Frauds and Scams

Suppliers

Telemarketers require suppliers of phone scripts, mailing lists, merchandise, phone banks, and autodialers (to dial prospects so that the callers never have to wait; there is always someone on the line). Mailing lists and phone lists sell for a few cents per name, with lists of the successfully scammed and good potential victims (those with bad credit records) renting for 10¢-15¢ a name.

Turnkeys

Turnkeys are operations that provide telemarketing scammers with a total package of services, from autodialers and prospect lists to credit card receipt and check laundering to merchandise. The scammers make sure that their merchandise is valued at just under $300, the threshold at which postal inspectors are required to investigate for fraud. But legitimate organizations often become involved, such as the phone companies and post office.

Reputable banks often turn down telemarketers' requests for credit card services because of their high number of "chargebacks": refusals to pay particular charges on a credit card. Card issuers lose millions of dollars a year to chargebacks from phone fraud, because federal law gives consumers 60 days to protest a charge, which if successful, must be absorbed by the card issuer. Unable to obtain credit card services from banks on their own, telemarketers hire "independent service organizations" which approach banks on their behalf, offering to protect the bank from chargebacks by getting the telemarketer to post a large bond to cover potential losses. But even a half-million-dollar bond reserve can be quickly depleted by chargebacks, leaving the service company and bank with enormous losses.

Factoring Companies

Telemarketing operations also commonly engage "factoring" companies, firms that buy credit card receipts from telemarketing concerns at a discount, then use their merchant bank accounts to convert the receipts into cash. Some factors charge as much as 30% of gross receipts' value to launder the slips. Factoring is illegal in some states, but crooks find loophole to slip through, or disguise their alliances. International factoring companies.

Factoring through Asian and European merchants is becoming increasingly common. These foreign concerns tend to charge less than American factors at 9%-10% of the gross. Factors can make big profits wherever they are but risk banks freezing their accounts or suing them for too many chargebacks. In response to losses suffered from dishonest telemarketers, banks and credit card companies now review their accounts to locate those businesses with inordinate numbers of chargebacks and close these accounts, even filing suit if they can find the account holder. However, an international factor may use a bank in its own country that will not do as you say.

MASTERING INTERNAL CONTROLS AND FRAUD PREVENTION

Instructions: Detach the Final Examination Answer Sheet on page 91 before beginning the final exam. Select the letter for the correct answer to each multiple-choice question below and mark it on the Answer Sheet. Allow approximately 1 hour.

1. The greatest vulnerability to inventory theft is having . . .

    a. a dishonest employee.
    b. insufficient controls on shipping reports.
    c. no centralized department for receiving and storing merchandise.
    d. insufficient controls on purchasing.

2. A red flag that indicates that an inventory theft scheme operating within your company is:

    a. an increase in accounts receivable as a percentage of sales
    b. an increase in Cost Of Goods Sold as a percentage of sales
    c. an increase in accounts payable as a percentage of costs
    d. an decrease in accounts receivable as a percentage of sales

3. Which of the following may be red flags of an inventory theft scheme operating within your company?

    a. Shipments of merchandise for which there is no record of a sale
    b. A higher number of uncollectible sales or greater bad debt expense
    c. Sales are canceled after merchandise is shipped
    d. Any of the above

4. Which of the following is a control designed to prevent inventory theft?

    a. Prenumbered and controlled requisitions, receiving reports, inventory tags and sales tickets
    b. Making sure that the same employee who receives inventory also does the year-end physical count of inventory
    c. Making sure that the employee who keeps the ledger inventory accounts also does the year-end physical count of inventory
    d. Having one employee control shipping, receiving, and inventory records

5. Which of the following duties should be handled by different personnel whenever possible?

    a. Requisition, control, and disbursement of inventory
    b. Requisition of inventory and conversion of inventory to scrap
    c. Requisition, receipt, and control of inventory
    d. All of the above

6. Which of the following is a tool used in an analytical review of inventory to see if inventory is being stolen?

    a. Subtracting Cost Of Goods Sold from net sales, dividing the result by net sales, then comparing the result to the same ratio for prior periods
    b. Dividing Cost Of Goods Sold by average inventory and comparing the result to that of prior years
    c. Both a and b
    d. Neither a nor b

7. The question about a job applicant that is likeliest to elicit a useful answer from previous employers is:

    a. Did this person ever attempt to steal anything from you?
    b. Is this person eligible for rehire?
    c. Do you think that this person is honest?
    d. Would you recommend that we hire this person?

8. Before checking references or other pre-employment information, you should consult with a lawyer or HR specialist and . . .

    a. inform the applicant that you are doing so.
    b. get the applicant's oral consent to do so.
    c. get the applicant's written consent to do so.
    d. make sure the applicant does not know you are checking pre-employment information, so that he/she cannot forewarn references or others you may contact..

9. A fraud audit should include a review of . . .

    a. expense reports, payroll records, and purchasing records by a person who does not normally handle these records.
    b. requisitions, shipping documents, sales records, and remittance advices by someone who does not normally handle these records.
    c. Accounts Receivable, customer complaints, and suspense accounts by someone who does not normally handle these areas..
    d. all of the above.

10. Which of the following are optional additions on a fidelity bond?

    a. Losses from counterfeit paper currency or money orders

    b. Losses from forged deposits or forged credit cards

    c. Losses from computer forgery

    d. All of the above

11. In a company with 1-5 employees, an effective way to prevent employee fraud involving company checks or bank accounts is to . . .

    a. have all bank statements and checks sent directly to the owner's home.

    b. have the owner or his/her spouse shuffle the checks so that employees will know that someone is checking the monthly bank statement but will not know the level of review.

    c. both a and b.

    d. neither a nor b.

12. When the owner's spouse works at the office, you should . . .

    a. brief the spouse on internal controls after all of the meetings on internal controls are over.

    b. make sure that the spouse is at the first meeting on internal controls and take special precautions if an employee ever replaces the spouse.

    c. not involve the spouse because spouses tend to be too trusting of employees.

    d. not involve the spouse because they have no interest in internal controls.

13. Based on experience, which of the following are the most common signs that someone may be trying to pass counterfeit travelers' checks?

    a. You are given one check for $100 and the passer wants most of it back in cash.

    b. You are given five checks for $20 each and the passer buys a group of unrelated items.

    c. You are given several checks for any denomination and the passer buys the least appealing item(s) in the store.

    d. None of the above because experience shows that there are no typical patterns involved in passing counterfeit travelers' checks.

14. When you ask for company checks to be made with scrambled indicia, you are asking the check producer to create . . .

  a. a pattern of colors that are difficult to separate, even with special cameras, filters, and film.
  b. a random pattern of colored dots printed on the paper that, when viewed though a colored filter, appear as a word or pattern.
  c. what appears to be a solid line that, under a magnifying glass, is several very small words or letters that are very difficult to recreate with a normal printing process.
  d. a seal on the back of checks that appears when held up to light.

15. What are the most practical, effective steps to take to spot forgery involving company checks returned with the company bank statement?

  a. Examine each check's routing number and endorsement and verify each check's dollar amount against the check register.
  b. Fan the checks looking for any with a slightly different color, verify each check's dollar amount against the check register, and investigate any gap if check numbers are not consecutive.
  c. Fan the checks looking for any with a slightly different color and investigate if there are unusual gaps in consecutive check numbers or too many checks with second endorsements.
  d. Hold each check up to the light or under a magnifying glass to check each one's hologram or other special printing technique.

16. Which of the following may be signs of payroll fraud?

  a. A second endorsement on an employee's paycheck or a different endorsement from the one you normally see
  b. An employee not present when paychecks are delivered
  c. No timecard for an employee or a timecard filled out in a supervisor's handwriting or that has different looking signatures
  d. All of the above

17. When checking the identification of a customer who wants to pay by check, employees should accept . . .

  a. two photo i.d.s such as a valid driver's license or other state i.d. signed by the customer and with recent photos.
  b. any two signed laminated i.d.s with recent photos.
  c. at least one i.d. signed by the customer with a recent photo and a Social Security card, birth certificate or insurance card.
  d. any of the above.

18. Which of the following should cause the employee to examine a check more closely or call a supervisor:

    a. a check number under 300 with perforated edges and a customer who dashes off the signature.

    b. a customer who buys expensive items, complains about the service and does not ask if there is a minimum required to pay by check.

    c. a check on which the transit number in the top right corner matches the electronically encoded number at the bottom of the check.

    d. a check number under 200 with smooth edges and a customer who signs the check slowly and with great care.

19. Which of the following is the most important step for employees to take on a credit card transaction to protect against credit card fraud?

    a. Check the hologram on the credit card for the correct colors.

    b. Compare the signatures on the credit card and charge-card sales slip.

    c. Verify the expiration date on the credit card.

    d. Refuse the sale if the card is unsigned, even if the customer offers to sign it in front of the employee.

20. Employees should call a supervisor when a customer:

    a. makes several purchases with little regard for size, quality, or cost.

    b. charges expensive items on a newly valid credit card.

    c. cannot provide a photo i.d. when asked and rushes the employee.

    d. all of the above.

21. A valid "Visa" or "MasterCard" should have a signature panel with . . .

    a. "Visa" or "MasterCard" printed many times and numbers slanted left that match part or all of the account number on the front of the card.

    b. nothing on it but the signature and numbers slanted left that match part or all of the account number on the front of the card.

    c. nothing on it but the signature and numbers slanted right that match part or all of the account number on the front of the card.

    d. "Visa" or "MasterCard" printed many times but no numbers.

22. A valid American Express card should have

    a. a signature panel with wavy black lines, and a card number that begins with 43 or 47.

    b. a signature panel with wavy black lines, and a card number that begins with 34 or 37.

    c. a signature panel with wavy black lines, and a card number that begins with 4 or 5.

    d. a plain white signature panel, and a card number that begins with 34 or 37.

23. Company policy for company-issued employee credit cards should . . .

    a. permit employees to charge personal items on the card, then automatically deduct the amount(s) from the employee's paycheck.

    b. permit company-authorized personal items to be charged on the card and require prompt reimbursement from the employee.

    c. permit personal items to be charged on the card, then automatically deduct the amount plus processing fees from the employee's paycheck.

    d. prohibit personal items from being charged on the company card ,regardless of need or circumstances.

24. Company policy for company-issued employee credit cards should . . .

    a. permit the charge card statement and receipt to be used in place of normal vendor documentation.

    b. permit the charge card statement to be used in place of both the signed credit-card receipt and vendor documentation.

    c. require vendor documentation be submitted and accept the charge card statement and receipt only as proof that payment was made.

    d. allow any of the policies above because all are equally valid.

25. To avoid company liability for purchases made on stolen company credit cards, company policy should require that an employee whose card is lost or stolen . . .

    a. report the loss of the card within 10 days.

    b. report the loss of the card within 7 days.

    c. report the loss of the card within 5 days.

    d. report the loss of the card within 3 days.

26. Employees acting as agents for their employer—e.g., when making purchasing decisions—are legally required to . . .

    a. act in the employer's best interests.

    b. refrain from self-dealing or using their position to further their personal interests at the employer's expense.

    c. accept something of value to influence or base a business decision on the employee's best interests instead of the employer's.

    d. all of the above.

27. Telemarketers from a legitimate vendor . . .

    a. call only between 8 a.m. and 9 p.m.

    b. clearly identify themselves and their enterprise and provide a phone number where they can be reached so that, if you are interested in the offer, you can hang up and dial the number

    c. provide certain services and information before demanding payment and provide the details of the offer in a clearly stated or written form before the sales is closed

    d. all of the above

28. If your firm has ever been the victim of a telemarketing scam . . .

    a. it is likely to be the target of more scams.

    b. it is unlikely to be the target of more scams.

    c. it may or may not be the target of more scams; there is no pattern.

    d. any of the above.

29. If your firm is short of cash and a telemarketer happens to call offering your firm a loan, you should. . .

    a. check it out because your firm has nothing to lose.

    b. first go to your company's regular bank before considering a loan from an unfamiliar source.

    c. consider it if it is offered regardless of your firm's credit problems..

    d. seriously consider any source of a loan if your firm needs cash.

30. Which of the following statements is correct?

    a. For a list of current fraud scams, visit the FBI's Web site.

    b. To see how many fraud or other complaints a vendor has had and whether the complaints were resolved, visit the Better Business Bureau's Web site.

    c. For a list of telemarketing, Internet, and other frauds by type and frequency, visit the National Fraud Information Center Web site.

    d. All of the above.

This page left blank intentionally.

Final Examination Answer Sheet

MASTERING INTERNAL CONTROLS AND FRAUD PREVENTION

Instructions: Detach this sheet before starting your final examination. Select the letter of the correct answer for each question, then fill in the parallel lines (‖) right beneath that letter. Please use a #2 pencil to make a dark impression. When completed, return to: AIPB Continuing Education, Suite 500, 6001 Montrose Road, Rockville, MD 20852. If you achieve a grade of at least 70, you will receive the Institute's *Certificate of Completion.* Final Examinations are not returned.

For *Certified Bookkeeper* applicants only: If you achieve a grade of at least 70, and become a *Certified Bookkeeper* within three (3) years of passing this exam, you will receive retroactively three (3) Continuing Professional Education Credits (CPECs) toward your *Certified Bookkeeper* continuing education requirements.

1. a b c d	11. a b c d	21. a b c d
2. a b c d	12. a b c d	22. a b c d
3. a b c d	13. a b c d	23. a b c d
4. a b c d	14. a b c d	24. a b c d
5. a b c d	15. a b c d	25. a b c d
6. a b c d	16. a b c d	26. a b c d
7. a b c d	17. a b c d	27. a b c d
8. a b c d	18. a b c d	28. a b c d
9. a b c d	19. a b c d	29. a b c d
10. a b c d	20. a b c d	30. a b c d

Name (Please print clearly)   Title

Company   Street address

City   State   Zip

For *Certified Bookkeeper* applicants only: #_____
                          Membership or Certification ID number (for nonmembers)

NOTES

Course Evaluation for

MASTERING INTERNAL CONTROLS AND FRAUD PREVENTION

Please complete (even if you do not take the Final Examination) and return to: AIPB Continuing Education, Suite 500, 6001 Montrose Road, Rockville, MD 20852. **PLEASE PRINT CLEARLY.**

Circle one

1. Did you find the instructions clear?　　　　　　　　　　　　　　　　Yes　　　No

Comments: _____

_____

2. Did you find the course practical?　　　　　　　　　　　　　　　　Yes　　　No

Comments: _____

_____

3. Is this course what you expected?　　　　　　　　　　　　　　　　Yes　　　No

Comments: _____

_____

4. Would you recommend this course to other accounting professionals?　　Yes　　　No

Comments: _____

_____

5. What did you like most about *Mastering Internal Controls and Fraud Prevention?* _____

_____

6. What would have made the course even more helpful? _____

_____

7. May we use your comments and name in advertising for the course?　　Yes　　　No

8. Would you be interested in other courses?　　　　　　　　　　　　Yes　　　No

Please indicate what subject areas would be of greatest interest to you:

1. _____　　3. _____

2. _____　　4. _____

_____

Name (optional)　　　　　　　　　　　　Title

_____

Company　　　　　　　　　　　　　　　Street Address

_____

City　　　　　　State　　　　　　Zip　　　(____) _____　Phone no.

NOTES